Context and Communication

CONTEMPORARY INTRODUCTIONS TO
PHILOSOPHY OF LANGUAGE

Context and Communication

Herman Cappelen and Josh Dever

OXFORD
UNIVERSITY PRESS

OXFORD
UNIVERSITY PRESS

Great Clarendon Street, Oxford, OX2 6DP,
United Kingdom

Oxford University Press is a department of the University of Oxford.
It furthers the University's objective of excellence in research, scholarship,
and education by publishing worldwide. Oxford is a registered trade mark of
Oxford University Press in the UK and in certain other countries

© Herman Cappelen and Josh Dever 2016

The moral rights of the authors have been asserted

First Edition published in 2016

Impression: 1

All rights reserved. No part of this publication may be reproduced, stored in
a retrieval system, or transmitted, in any form or by any means, without the
prior permission in writing of Oxford University Press, or as expressly permitted
by law, by licence or under terms agreed with the appropriate reprographics
rights organization. Enquiries concerning reproduction outside the scope of the
above should be sent to the Rights Department, Oxford University Press, at the
address above

You must not circulate this work in any other form
and you must impose this same condition on any acquirer

Published in the United States of America by Oxford University Press
198 Madison Avenue, New York, NY 10016, United States of America

British Library Cataloguing in Publication Data

Data available

Library of Congress Control Number: 2015956473

ISBN 978-0-19-876991-0 (hbk)
978-0-19-873306-5 (pbk)

Printed in Great Britain by
Clays Ltd, St Ives plc

Links to third party websites are provided by Oxford in good faith and
for information only. Oxford disclaims any responsibility for the materials
contained in any third party website referenced in this work.

Contents

Detailed Contents	vii
Acknowledgment	xi
Introduction	1

Part I. Context Sensitivity: Variability vs. Stability — 5

1. Contextual Variability — 7
2. Stability Across Contexts — 32
3. Some Strategies for Reconciling Stability and Variability — 41

Part II. Theories of Context Sensitivity — 63

4. What is a Theory of Meaning? — 65
5. Character and Content — 86
6. Indexed Truth Accounts: An Alternative to Kaplan — 105
7. The Problem of Rigidity: Double Indexing and Monsters — 121
8. The Problem of Same-Saying: Two Strategies — 133

Part III. Contexts: What They Are and How We Create Them — 151

9. What are Contexts? — 153
10. More on Contextual Ingredients — 164
11. How Speech Creates Contexts: Negotiation and Accommodation — 177

Bibliography	191
Index	197

Detailed Contents

Acknowledgment	xi
Introduction	1

Part I. Context Sensitivity: Variability vs. Stability — 5

1. Contextual Variability — 7
   1.1 The Basic Cases: Variability and Stability — 7
   1.2 Context Sensitivity Beyond the Basic Set — 11
   1.3 Radical Contextualism: The View that Every Word is Context Sensitive — 22

2. Stability Across Contexts — 32
   2.1 Where We Are and the Plan for This Chapter — 32
   2.2 Three Arguments for Stability — 32

3. Some Strategies for Reconciling Stability and Variability — 41
   3.1 Where We Are and the Plan for This Chapter — 41
   3.2 Stability is an Illusion — 42
   3.3 Contextual Parasites — 45
   3.4 Minimalistic Pluralism — 50

Part II. Theories of Context Sensitivity — 63

4. What is a Theory of Meaning? — 65
   4.1 Where We Are and the Plan for This Chapter — 65
   4.2 What Are We Trying to Do with a Theory Of Meaning? — 66
   4.3 What is Said and Truth Conditions — 66
   4.4 Possible Worlds — 68
   4.5 Compositionality — 71
   4.6 Truth and Consequences — 75
   4.7 Rigidity — 77
   4.8 Semantics and Pragmatics — 79

5. Character and Content — 86
   5.1 Where We Are and the Plan for This Chapter — 86
   5.2 Kaplanian Theory of Meaning — 87
   5.3 Philosophical Payoffs of the Character–Content Distinction — 89
   5.4 Monsters and Rigidity — 96

6. Indexed Truth Accounts: An Alternative to Kaplan   105
   6.1 Where We Are and the Plan for This Chapter   105
   6.2 Kaplan, Content, and the Operator Argument   106
   6.3 Indexed Truth Theories   110
   6.4 Two Problems for Indexed Truth Accounts   114

7. The Problem of Rigidity: Double Indexing and Monsters   121
   7.1 Where We Are and the Plan for This Chapter   121
   7.2 Fixing the Problem of Rigidity with Double Indexing   122
   7.3 Character, Content, and Double Indexing   124
   7.4 Are Monsters Evidence for Double Indexing?   126

8. The Problem of Same-Saying: Two Strategies   133
   8.1 Where We Are and the Plan for This Chapter   133
   8.2 Lewis' Same-Saying Skepticism   134
   8.3 Stalnaker and Contextual Subjectivism   138
   8.4 Stalnaker, Updates, and Diagonals   142
   8.5 Stalnaker and Dynamic Pragmatics   146
   8.6 Final Thoughts on Formal Theorizing   147

Part III. Contexts: What They Are and How We Create Them   151

9. What are Contexts?   153
   9.1 Where We Are and the Plan for This Chapter   153
   9.2 Demonstratives and Context   155
   9.3 Improper Contexts   160

10. More on Contextual Ingredients   164
    10.1 Where We Are and the Plan for This Chapter   164
    10.2 Gradable Adjectives   165
    10.3 Epistemic 'Mights'   168
    10.4 You: Audience Sensitivity?   169
    10.5 Presupposition   171

11. How Speech Creates Contexts: Negotiation and Accommodation   177
    11.1 Where We Are and the Plan for This Chapter   177
    11.2 Lewis on Accommodation and Black Magic   177
    11.3 When We Don't Accommodate: Negotiation   180
    11.4 Why We Negotiate Over Meanings   181
    11.5 Meaning Negotiation and Asymmetrical Power Relations   184

 11.6 Asymmetrical Power Relations, Gender, Silencing,
   and Pornography   185
 11.7 Negotiation and Accommodation   188

Bibliography   191
Index   197

Acknowledgment

We would like to thank Matthew McKeever and Joshua Habgood-Coote for invaluable research assistance. We are also grateful to Brian Rabern for trying out an early version of the book on his students and giving us feedback, to Dilip Ninan and Torfinn Huveness for advice along the way. We got helpful comment from three anonymous referees for OUP. Finally, we got good feedback from students in St Andrews and Oslo who also used the book for their philosophy of language classes.

Introduction

This book is about the various ways in which what we say (and assert, ask, and think) depends on the context of speech and thought. The period since 1970 has produced a vast literature on this topic, both by philosophers and linguists. It is arguably the area of philosophy (and linguistics) where most progress has been made over the last forty years. The goal of this book is to provide students with an introduction to some of the central data, questions, concepts, and theories of context sensitivity.

The 'some' part of the previous sentence is important. This book is *not* meant to be exhaustive. The amount of work done by philosophers and linguists on this topic is immense. To cover it all, we would have had to write an extremely long and unwieldy book. So we don't aspire to comprehensiveness. Instead, we have picked some topics, views, and arguments that we think are important, interesting, and instructive. Our hope is that a reader who has understood and engaged with this selection of material will be in a good position to start engaging with much of the work we don't cover in this book.

The book is written to be accessible to someone with no prior knowledge of the material or, indeed, any prior knowledge of philosophy. It can be used as part of a philosophy of language course or as part of a general introduction to philosophy.

We initially set out to write a single book that could serve as an introduction to philosophy of language. We gave up. We now think that goal is too ambitious for any one book. There is simply too much interesting work done within this field over the last 100 years to cover it all (or even most of it) in a single book. A book that tried to do that would inevitably be so superficial that it would fail to convey to the readers how rich, complex, and important these topics are. To do justice to the field we have set out to write a series of introductions to philosophy of language, each one covering an important topic, each one of which would be a way into the field as a whole. These books aim to provide systematic introductions to important questions, data, theories, and arguments. Those looking for a history of the discipline should look elsewhere.

Here is an overview of the various chapters, and a guide to how to read the book.

Part I. Context Sensitivity: Variability vs. Stability

The first part concerns how to reconcile two facts about language and language use. On the one hand, most of the words we use appear to be sensitive to the context of speech. What we say to each other is shaped by the contexts we are in in when we speak, in ways that are complex and difficult to understand. On the other hand, language is a device for transmitting and storing information. If the information we get and transmit is sensitive to context in ways that are massively complicated and hard to understand, it is difficult to see how information can be shared between different contexts. The more we focus on the context sensitivity of what we say, the more it looks like what we say ends up being tied to the context of speech and it becomes hard to see how that information is moved between contexts. The first chapter in Part I outlines the evidence of context sensitivity. The second chapter outlines the arguments and evidence for stability between contexts. The third chapter considers some of the proposals for how to reconcile variability and stability: how to ensure shared information across contexts despite massive context sensitivity.

Part II. Theories of Context Sensitivity

In the first part of this book, we focus primarily on a puzzle about *communication*. We begin with some observations about the meanings and truth values of sentences, but from there move on to discuss what people *say with* and *understand by* uses of those sentences. In the second part of the book, we turn to looking in more detail at what a theory of meaning for a language could be. Our main goal here is to set out and compare two major approaches to a theory of meaning for context-sensitive language, one originating in the work of David Kaplan and the other in David Lewis' work. The shift to thinking more about the functioning of language and less about the use of that language by speakers means that we will need to think in more detail about the *internal functioning* of the language: how the meanings of whole sentences are determined by the meanings of the words that make them up.

Part III. Contexts: What They Are and How We Create Them

Throughout this book, the notion of a context plays a central role. In the final part of the book we turn directly to the question of what a context is and how it does its work. We start by distinguishing two questions: (i) What is it to be in a context? (ii) How does context determine the meaning of words? We then consider two views of contexts to see how they can respond to these questions. We next turn to a more detailed discussion of what 'ingredients' a context must provide to account for gradable adjectives like 'rich', the second-person pronoun 'you', and other expressions. In the final chapter, we consider how speech itself can create contexts, how contextual accommodation and negotiation works, and how asymmetric power relations affect contextual negotiations. We conclude the book by presenting a radical line of thought: because to negotiate over what the word 'legal' means is to negotiate over what is or should be legal, contextual negotiation is not just negotiation over the meaning of words, but also about what the world is or should be like.

PART I

Context Sensitivity: Variability vs. Stability

The first three chapters of this book should be thought of as a continuous argument.

- In this first chapter we sketch a case for the view that natural language is massively context sensitive. By that we mean, roughly (and pre-theoretically) that what is said by an utterance depends on the context in which it is uttered (i.e. it depends on the speaker, the audience, the time, the place, the conversational context, etc.). Maybe, in some significant sense, every single sentence of natural language exhibits context sensitivity of this kind.
- In the second chapter we present arguments and data that purport to show that context sensitivity *cannot* be widespread. It cannot be widespread, we'll suggest, because that would make language useless for preserving and transmitting information. That, after all, is an essential function of language.

So the first two chapters should leave the readers puzzled: there are good arguments both that language is massively context sensitive, and that it can't be. Which are right?

- The third chapter is an introduction to various views that attempt to resolve this puzzle.

1
Contextual Variability

This first chapter has two broad goals.

First, it introduces the idea of linguistic context sensitivity through a series of examples. The rest of the book will introduce more technical vocabulary for describing what goes on in these cases, but for the purposes of this chapter, we try to keep the theory to a minimum.

Second, we try to make clear why understanding context sensitivity is important. There are two basic sources of significance.

(i) On the one hand, it is *extrinsically* significant: it has wide-reaching consequences for other fields of philosophy. It is not much of an exaggeration to say that in every field of philosophy, questions about context sensitivity are of fundamental significance. However, the broader implications are not limited to philosophy. What you think about this topic will fundamentally influence how you should think about moral, political, social, and legal issues. Our initial series of examples will make this clear.

(ii) On the other hand, the challenge of trying to understand the ways context shapes thought is one of the most *intrinsically* interesting topics philosophers have grappled with over the last 100 years. Most of this book is an introduction to those intellectual challenges.

1.1 The Basic Cases: Variability and Stability

Here are some "What is X?" questions that philosophers have struggled with for more than 2000 years:

- What is love?
- What is it to be good?

- What is causation?
- What is knowledge?
- What is truth?
- What is rationality?
- What is happiness?
- What is logical consequence?
- What is it for something to be possible?
- What is it for something to have a color? (e.g. to be red)
- What is the right thing to do?
- What is friendship?

Arguably, the answer to all these questions (and practically every other question of that general form) is, in part: "Well, that depends on the context". *If that is right, then understanding context sensitivity is one of the most important challenges facing someone trying to gain philosophical understanding, or, indeed, any understanding of anything.*

To see why it is true, we need to understand what 'context sensitivity' means. Any attempt to answer that question will start with the simplest cases—the cases we understand best. Consider utterances of 'I am happy' and 'John left yesterday'.

1. Jill utters 'I am happy'.
2. Alex utters 'I am happy'.
3. Nora utters 'John left yesterday' on Monday.
4. Sofia utters 'John left yesterday' on Tuesday.

Here are four facts about these utterances:

(i) **They involve variability in reference:** If Jill utters 'I am happy', she uses 'I' to say something about herself. One important function of the word 'I' in Jill's utterance is to pick out Jill. In what follows, we use the term 'reference' for this phenomenon. We will say that *Jill is using 'I' to refer to herself*, i.e. to Jill. If Alex utters 'I am happy', she says about herself, i.e. Alex, that she is happy. So the word 'I' will refer to different people depending on who utters the sentence. Note that 'yesterday' also varies its reference, depending not on who is speaking but on the time of the utterance: in Nora's utterance 'yesterday' will refer to Sunday. In Sofia's utterance that same word will refer to Monday.

(ii) **They involve variability in 'what is said'**: Suppose someone asked you what Jill said when she uttered 'I am happy'. That question might at first seem a bit weird, but the simple and obvious answer would be that she said about herself—i.e. about Jill—that she is happy. What did Alex say when she uttered 'I am happy'? She said that Alex is happy. So what they say is different; they utter the same sentence, but what they say isn't the same. Think of this as a corollary of the difference in what was referred to: What is said depends on what is referred to. Since the two occurrences of 'I' in the two utterances refer to different people, what is said is different. The same can be said about Nora and Sofia: what Nora said was that John left on Sunday. What Sofia said was that John left on Monday. Again, what is said varies as the result of variability in what is referred to.

(iii) **They involve variability in truth value**: It is possible for Jill's utterance to be true, but Alex's utterance to be false. If Jill is, in fact, happy, but Alex isn't, then what Jill says is true and what Alex says isn't. Sentences have *truth values*. If a sentence is true, its truth value is *true*; if it is false, its truth value is *false*. You can think of the variability in truth value in part as a corollary of the variability in what was referred to and what was said: differences in what was said can lead to differences in truth value. If Jill and Alex said exactly the same thing, then what they said would have to agree in truth value. Note that we have the same potential variability with respect to Nora and Sofia: if John in fact left on Sunday and not on Monday, then what Nora is said is true and what Sofia said is false.

(iv) **They involve stability in form**: There is, however, one obvious point of stability. The sentencs themselves ('I am happy' and 'John left yesterday'). We have (potential) variability in reference, in what was said, and in truth value, but stability in the words used.

Our language contains many words that are like 'I' and 'yesterday' in these respects. Consider two utterances of 'The meeting starts now'. Each occurrence of 'now' will pick out the time at which it is uttered. They will, in the terminology introduced earlier, *refer to* the time at which they are uttered. As a result, we can get the three kinds of variability mentioned above. (i) Variability in reference: If they are uttered at different times, the two utterances of 'now' refer to different times. (ii) Variability in what was said: If the first one is uttered at noon, then 'now' refers to noon and the speaker says that the meeting starts at noon. If the second is uttered at 1pm, then 'now' refers to 1pm, and the utterance will say that the meeting starts at 1pm. (iii) Variability in truth value: If the meeting starts at noon, what is said in the first speech is true and what is said in the second is false.

Consider two utterances of 'You are wearing a red hat'. An utterance of 'you' refers to the speaker's audience. If we vary the audience, we get varied referents. If in the first context the audience is Jill, then the speaker is saying that Jill is wearing a red hat. If in the second context the audience is Naomi, the speaker is saying that Naomi is wearing a red hat. If Jill, but not Naomi, is wearing a red hat, then the first utterance is true and the second utterance is false.

Other words that exhibit these kinds of variability (combined with stability in form) include 'today', 'yesterday', 'tomorrow', etc., 'here', 'there', 'that', 'we', 'she', 'he', 'us', and 'it'. We will call this rough category the *Basic Set*.

1.1.1 Contexts

So far we've talked about three kinds of variability (in reference, what is said, and truth value) and one kind of stability (in the form of the sentence). What's the source of the variability? The answer is twofold. In part it is determined by the meaning of the words: they are the kinds of words whose meaning in the language (i.e. in English) requires this variability. In part, the variability is a result of some aspect of the speech situation. Which aspect of the speech situation that matters varies between the examples above: for 'I' it is the identity of the speaker that matters; for 'you', the audience; for 'now', the time of speech; for 'that', the object demonstrated; and so on. The meaning of a context-sensitive word will, in some sense, *tell* you what the relevant feature of the speech situation is. To be able to talk more generally about this, we will, in these initial chapters, use the term 'context' to refer collectively to those features of the speech situation that make reference vary (e.g. speaker, audience, demonstrated object, time, place etc.). So by *context* we mean all those things, whatever they may be, that trigger such variability in context-sensitive expressions. In Chapter 8, we will consider more detailed theories about what sorts of things contexts are. For now, we will operate with this pre-theoretic notion.

1.2 Context Sensitivity Beyond the Basic Set

So far we've pointed out something fairly obvious: words like 'I', 'now', 'here', and 'that' vary their referents depending on context. There are interesting and complicated theoretical questions about how that fact can be accommodated in a systematic theory of meaning. Those issues are explored in Chapters 4–8. In this first part of the book, we continue to explore the data. As mentioned in the introductory paragraph, the data about context sensitivity is complex and important because it touches on the nature of almost everything we care about in this world. In what follows, we present a selection of cases to illustrate this.

1.2.1 *Legal contexts: the context sensitivity of 'use a firearm' and 'all citizens are equal before the law'*

The correct interpretation of laws has wide-ranging practical consequences. The job of a judge is, in part, to interpret the law. More often than not the correct interpretations of laws (or the words used to formulate the laws) depend on context. To illustrate this, philosophers of law often talk about a case known as *Smith vs United States*, and, in particular, about some points Supreme Court Justice Antonin Scalia makes in his dissent to the court's ruling on that case. The statute in the case is this:

[A]ny person who...uses or carries a firearm [in the course of committing a crime of violence or drug trafficking] shall, in addition to the punishment provided for such [a] crime...be sentenced to a term of imprisonment of not less than five years. (18 U.S.C. § 924(c) (1))

Smith was found guilty of drug trafficking. He had traded his gun for illegal drugs. Keep in mind that he didn't use the gun as a weapon. *It was in a plastic bag and was handed over in exchange for the drugs.* So here is an important question: what does 'uses a firearm' mean in the context of that law? The court found that Smith had *used a firearm in the course of committing the crime* and so was subject to the more stringent sentencing—he had to serve five extra years.

Justice Scalia, in his dissent, can be seen grappling with the very issues this book is about. Here is, in part, Scalia's objection:

To use an instrumentality ordinarily means to use it for its intended purpose. When someone asks "Do you use a cane?" he is not inquiring whether you have your grandfather's silver-handled walking stick on display in the hall; he wants to know whether you *walk* with a cane. Similarly, to speak of "using a firearm" is to speak of using it for its distinctive purpose, i.e., as a weapon. To be sure, "one can use a firearm in a number of ways," *ante*, at 7, including as an article of exchange, just as one can "use" a cane as a hall decoration... (Smith vs The United States, 508 U.S. at 242 (Scalia, J., dissenting))

Scalia observes that 'Smith used a firearm' can be used to mean many different things—used it to scratch his head, as a wall decoration, as a hammer, as a doorstop, or as an article of exchange. However, Scalia argues, this fact does not justify adding five years to Smith's sentence because, according to Scalia:

The Court does not appear to grasp the distinction between how a word *can be* used and how it *ordinarily is* used. It would, indeed, be "both reasonable and normal to say that petitioner 'used' his MAC-10 in his drug trafficking offense by trading it for cocaine." *Ibid*. It would also be reasonable and normal to say that he "used" it to scratch his head. When one wishes to describe the action of employing the instrument of a firearm for such unusual purposes, "use" is assuredly a verb one could select. But that says nothing about whether the *ordinary* meaning of the phrase "uses a firearm" embraces such extraordinary employments. **It is unquestionably *not* reasonable and normal, I think, to say simply "do not use firearms" when one means to prohibit selling or scratching with them.** (Emphasis added.)(Smith vs The United States, 508 U.S. at 242 (Scalia, J., dissenting))

According to Scalia, in legal contexts, we should interpret the occurrence of words according to their 'reasonable and normal' use. The other uses are, according to Scalia, irrelevant to the interpretation of the statute. So Smith, according to Scalia, should be off the hook (or at least not get an extra five years). Not so, according to the majority in the Supreme Court. This textbook takes no stand on how Smith should be sentenced, but does note that whatever your view might be, it *should* be informed by an understanding of linguistic context sensitivity. More generally, an understanding of the law, legal interpretation, and how laws should be applied requires an understanding of linguistic context sensitivity. A theory of legal interpretation that is *not* embedded in a more general theory of linguistic context sensitivity is necessarily incomplete and uninformed.

It should be clear that this point generalizes very widely. We include only one more law-related illustration. In a much-cited passage from a dissent in "Plessy v. Fergurson" (163 U.S. 537 (1896)), it says: "... all citizens are equal before the law". Now imagine two utterances of that sentence, one in the context of a class on the US constitution and another in a course on sociology. You might think it true in the first context (as a generalization over how the law *ought* to treat citizens), but false in the second (as a generalization over how *as a matter of fact* different groups are treated).

1.2.2 The context sensitivity of 'love' and love

First, a clarification of the strange heading. Why talk about both the word 'love' and love itself? This book is about language, so shouldn't our focus be on the word 'love', and not love itself? Our primary concern is with the word and its context sensitivity. One way to test for that is to check whether there are two different speech contexts such that 'A loves B' is true in one but not in the other. In so doing, we change nothing about A and B and their relationship, but change only the conversational context. We present a case like that below as evidence that 'love' is context sensitive. Now, note that if 'love' is context sensitive, then, in some important sense, *what love is* is also context sensitive. After all, love is the thing that the word 'love' picks out. If that word picks out different kinds of relationships in different contexts, then love is all those relationships—unless we have reason to think one of those contexts picks out 'true love' (and that is the only thing truly worthy of the label 'love'). More generally, if an expression E is context sensitive, then in some important sense the question: *What is E?* has as part of its answer, *That depends on context.* If the data in the rest of this chapter is right, then a lot of things depend on context.

So, now to the question: Is 'love' context sensitive? Consider the following two contexts, Low-Standard Love Context and High-Standard Love Context:

Low-Standard Love Context: After watching a movie, Jill says, "I love that actor".

High-Standard Love Context: Jill is asked, "What would you do to protect those you love?" In trying to answer, she makes a list of the people she loves. She says, "I love my children, my parents", and so on. Jill is then asked, "But don't you love that actor from the movie we saw yesterday? What would you do to protect him?" She answers, "No, I don't love him".

What these contrasting cases illustrate is that the threshold for when a relationship counts as a loving relationship can go up and down. In some contexts, it is easier for some state or relationship to count as love. In other contexts, it is more difficult. In simplistic terms: how much fondness or commitment needs to be present for a relationship to count as 'love' varies with context. This is simplistic for two reasons. First, love obviously isn't *simply* a matter of quantity of fondness and commitment. It is more complicated. That said, the general point remains: the degree of X varies between contexts (where X is whatever complex ingredients make up love). Second, it is simplistic because it assumes that the 'ingredients' of love must be stable across contexts, but there is reason to think that is false. Consider the question: *does Alex love Jill?* Suppose in one context, it is assumed that Jill is Alex's daughter, in another it is assumed she is her lover, in a third that she is a close friend. One plausible view is that in each of these contexts, different 'ingredients' are required for it to be the case that Alex loves Jill. So it is not just the degree of X that varies between contexts, it is also X itself.

> **Observation #1.1** *Context Sensitivity and Ambiguity*
>
> Context sensitivity is different from ambiguity. The word 'I' isn't typically described as ambiguous. This is because, in some important sense, the meaning of 'I' is stable between contexts, whereas ambiguous words vary their meaning. When you learn and understand 'I', you know that it is the kind of expression that can be used by different speakers to refer to themselves. You don't have to learn 'I' over again when you hear a new person use it. You know it refers to whomever that person is—that is what understanding 'I' amounts to. This is different from ambiguous words like 'bank'. If you've only learned that 'bank' can be used to refer to the things that border rivers, then there's no way for you to grasp its meaning when applied to a financial institution. Grasping that new meaning is like learning the meaning of a new word. 'Love' seems to fit the pattern of 'I': There's continuity between 1–4:
>
> 1. I love you (said to a child, a parent, a lover, a friend, or an idol).
> 2. I love Buenos Aires.
> 3. I love philosophy.
> 4. I love that actor.
>
> Neither of these requires re-learning 'love' in the way that encountering a new meaning for 'bank' does.

1.2.3 *Two dimensions of the context sensitivity of 'friend' and friendship*

'Friend' (and 'enemy') is context sensitive along at least two dimensions: To be a friend is to be a friend *of someone* and, in some contexts, we can leave that 'of...' component implicit and let the audience figure it out by context. That is the first dimension of context sensitivity.

The second dimension is this: What counts as a friend (or enemy) will vary between contexts—in somewhat the same way that what counts as love will vary between contexts. Consider the following two contexts, Low-Standard Friend Context and High-Standard Friend Context:

> **Low-Standard Context for Friend:** Consider a four-year old, Nora, in a playground. She meets another kid, Alex, and they play for a while. In this context, it is perfectly fine to say "Nora and Alex are friends", and it could be followed up by saying "Say goodbye to your friend" while leaving.

Observation #1.2 *Context Sensitivity and Vagueness*

Terms like 'friend', 'enemy', and 'child' are vague, but their vagueness should not be confused with their context sensitivity. To see both the difference and the connection between vagueness and context sensitivity, consider the term 'child'. That term is vague. There are people who are in between being a child and being an adult, and we wouldn't comfortably apply either term to them. One standard way to define 'vague term' is as a term that has such borderline cases. The meaning of the term 'child' is such that for many people, their age simply doesn't settle the matter of whether they are a child or not. That's vagueness, not context sensitivity.

Nonetheless, vague terms are always also context sensitive. Here is why. We often resolve vagueness in different ways in different contexts. In some contexts, a sixteen-year-old definitely counts as a child, in other contexts not. Here is Timothy Williamson's (2005: 99) succinct summary of this connection:

> We understand them (vague terms) not by learning precise definitions but by extrapolating from examples which leave their application to ranges of borderline cases unclear. In many contexts, speakers find it convenient to
>
> *(continued)*

> **Observation #1.2** *Continued*
>
>> resolve some of this vagueness in one way or another, according to their practical purposes. Naturally, they will sometimes find it convenient to resolve the vagueness in opposite ways in different contexts. One local stipulation about the extension of 'red' makes it include x; elsewhere, another local stipulation about the extension of 'red' makes it exclude x. Vague terms appear not to cut nature at the joints, not to pick up hidden but sharp and uniquely natural divisions into kinds that might stabilize their reference: . . . Of course, context relativity is not the very same phenomenon as vagueness: that 'I' refers to John as uttered by John and to Mary as uttered by Mary is an example of context relativity without being an example of vagueness. Nevertheless, one might think that the vagueness of a term makes contextual variation in its reference practically irresistible (even though it also makes the variation hard to measure).
>
> In sum, vagueness isn't the same as context sensitivity, but vagueness implies it. There is a lot of vagueness, and so there is a lot of context sensitivity.

High-Standard Context for Friend: Suppose while Nora plays with Alex, we are planning a small birthday party for her and making a list of her friends. It wouldn't be appropriate to list Alex and other playground acquaintances. In these contexts our standards go up, and more is required to count as a friend.

To put it loosely, how close and of what kind the relationship needs to be for A and B to count as friends will vary between contexts—closely analogously to how love varies across contexts. For more illustrations of such variability, consider the difference between a Facebook friend, a childhood friend, a close friend, and a workplace friend.

We're now going to consider several philosophically important cases of context sensitivity. Don't worry if you don't get every detail or their significance right away—we'll be coming back to some of these examples later in the book. Our point in this chapter is just illustrative: to show you the ubiquity of context sensitivity.

1.2.4 *Gradable adjectives and what it is to be good*

Gradable adjectives are those that can be used comparatively (e.g. 'Jill is taller than Alex, but Alex is richer than Jill') and where there's a superlative use of the adjective, e.g. 'tall*est*' and 'rich*est*'. Does being rich (or smart or fast or happy or sad) depend on the context? Almost everyone thinks the answer is 'yes'. In one context, you can say that Josh is fast because he runs marathons in under 3.30 hours. So, in many settings, it would be true to say "Josh is fast". However, when the topic is the speed of rockets or particles in accelerators or Olympic runners or leopards, it wouldn't be true to say 'Josh is fast' because, compared to any of those, he's not fast. It looks like, roughly, an occurrence of 'fast' is understood, in context, as 'fast for a . . . ' where the dots are filled in by something like a comparison class (i.e., a class of objects we compare Josh to—compared to the class of leopards Josh is not fast, but compared to the class of professional philosophers he's super fast). This comparison class is fixed in context. Alternatively, think of it like this: there's a scale of speed and the cutoff for what counts as fast varies between contexts.

It is not just the cutoff for what counts as fast that varies between contexts. When 'fast' is used by itself, we interpret it as 'fast at . . . ' where the dots are filled in by some activity. If someone says 'Josh is fast', you need to know what Josh is said to be fast at. It is typing, cooking, running, or grading? This is also fixed in context.

This has important consequence for moral terms and moral philosophy. Take the term 'good'. It is a gradable adjective (it is used comparatively: 'good', 'better', 'best'). When we describe something as good—an act or a person or an object—we therefore describe it as good relative to a comparison class or a cutoff point on a scale. The comparison class and the cutoff point are fixed in context and vary between contexts. Being good for a knife is different from being good for a dog, or a teacher, or a philosopher, or an astronaut, or a person. So it looks like we have a very quick route to some (weak) version of moral subjectivism or relativism. The claim 'Alex is good' or 'that was a good act' will depend on context in this sense: what is said by an utterance of either of these sentences depends on the comparison class (or scale) fixed in context. So the claim could be true in one context (given the comparison class/scale in that context), but false in another. So such claims can't be true or false independently of context. To avoid that conclusion, the opponent of moral relativism would have to show that the distinctively moral use of 'good' is different from other gradable adjectives. (Note that gradable adjectives will be discussed further in Chapter 9.)

1.2.5 Counterfactual conditionals

Counterfactuals are claims about what could have been the case. We *could* have written this book in China, but we didn't. As a matter of fact we wrote it in St Andrews, Austin, Toronto, and Oslo. Thoughts about what could have been the case are important for many aspects of life. They affect our practical reasoning and planning (a person takes out travel insurance because it *could be* the case that he or she will have an accident) and for how we evaluate what has happened (someone might be sad because she stayed at home when she *could have* gone to a party). The standard view in the philosophical literature is that claims (and thoughts) about what could have been the case depend on context. This is less obvious than the previous cases and the mechanism that triggers the context sensitivity is complicated (and still immensely controversial—much more so than, for example, the context sensitivity of 'I').

To see what philosophers have in mind when they say that counterfactual conditionals are context sensitive, consider the following example discussed by Goodman (1947), Quine (1960), and Lewis (1973). We are asked to consider some claims about what the Roman Emperor Julius Caesar would have done had he been in command of some contemporary American-led war (e.g. the war in Afghanistan). Lewis asks us to consider the following two counterfactuals:

1. If Caesar had been in command, he would have used the atom bomb.
2. If Caesar had been in command, he would have used catapults.

These claims, though they seem to contradict each other, can both be true, depending on context:

- How could 1 be true? It requires, speaking loosely, a context in which the speakers are focusing on Caesar's character (such as his brutality) and also keeping fixed what generals in Afghanistan know about weapons, etc. We are, so to speak, imagining how a modern-day version of Caesar, with full knowledge of modern weaponry, would command troops in Afghanistan.
- How could 2 be true? Suppose the focus of the conversation is on how a non-modernized Caesar, who lacks knowledge of modern weaponry, would command troops if he somehow found himself commanding troops in Afghanistan. In such contexts, 2 would strike us as true.

Describing just what varies between contexts in such cases is very controversial. Pre-theoretically, what varies is the facts we hold fixed, as we consider counterfactual scenarios. Somehow, context determines what background facts are relevant for assessing counterfactual claims.

1.2.6 Causation

Suppose Bob murders Jill by throwing her out the window of a tall building. We typically don't think of gravity as being the cause of death. Bob's act was the cause. Or suppose that upon hitting the ground, Jill broke her neck. We don't think of *her having a neck* as the cause of death. We don't say: oh, too bad she had a neck, if she had been neckless (or her neck was made from steel), she would have survived. One way to capture this is that we, pre-theoretically, distinguish between the cause of an action and the background conditions of the action. It has often been observed that *how* this distinction is drawn will depend on context. Hart and Honoré (1985: 35–6) is the classic exploration of this point:

The cause of a great famine in India may be identified by an Indian peasant as the drought, but the World Food Authority may identify the Indian Government's failure to build up food reserves as the cause and the drought as a mere condition.

As Menzies (2004: 144) points out, depending on context, we could judge both 1 and 2 true (but in no context are both true):

1. The drought caused the famine and the failure to stockpile food reserves was a mere background condition.
2. The failure to stockpile food reserves caused the famine and the drought was a mere background condition.

1 and 2 are inconsistent—they can't both be true. Nonetheless, answer 1 is true in one context and answer 2 in another context. So the correct answer to the question: "What caused the great famine in India?" will depend on the context you are in when you attempt to answer it. That is, in part, because the word 'cause' is context sensitive: What counts as a background condition and what as a cause varies between contexts.

1.2.7 'Might'

Some uses of 'might' are used to describe what is compatible with what we know:

1: Where is John?
2: He might be in his office.

A first stab at what B says is that for all he (i.e. B) knows, John is in his office. Roughly, B says he can't rule out that John is in his office. Is this use of 'might' (sometimes called an 'epistemic might') context dependent? The standard answer is 'yes'. Here is a context-shifting case from the linguist Angelika Kratzer (1991: 654):

> Suppose a man is approaching both of us. You are standing over there. I am further away. I can only see the bare outlines of the man. In view of my evidence, the person approaching may be Fred. You know better. In view of your evidence, it cannot possibly be Fred, it must be Martin. If this is so, my utterance of (1) and your utterance of (2) are both true.
> (1) The person approaching might be Fred.
> (2) The person approaching cannot be Fred.
> Had I uttered (2) and you (1), both our utterances would have been false.

Again, a familiar data pattern emerges. If Kratzer were to say "that might be Fred", then her utterance would be true. However, if her reader were to say "that might be Fred," then her utterance would be false (and vice versa for "that cannot be Fred"). One of them is true and the other is false. If so, what might be the case depends on context. For one speaker the person approaching might be Fred, for the other speaker, the person must be Martin and cannot be Fred. There is no inconsistency because what might be the case depends, at least at first glance, on the information state of the speaker. It depends, at least in part, on what you know. If you know that the person approaching is Martin, then you can't truly say "It might be Fred". But someone farther way, who knows less, can say "It might be Fred" and speak truly. (Note that epistemic 'might, will be discussed further in Chapter 9.)

1.2.8 The nature of knowledge and what someone knows

In the previous section, we said that what might be the case for you depends on what you know. But what about knowledge itself? Might that too be context sensitive? That question has been intensely discussed over the last thirty years. Does what it takes for someone to know something depend on context? Is the verb 'know' context sensitive? According to so-called contextualists about knowledge, the answer to these questions is 'yes'.

The motivation for contextualism about knowledge is more complicated than the previous cases. It is, in part, a data pattern of the kind that should by now be familiar. It is also engaged with larger theoretical considerations: For many contextualists, such as David Lewis (1996) and Stewart Cohen (1999), one motivation is that the position provides a way to respond to the skeptic. We'll go through these motivations in turn. First, a case that provides evidence for context sensitivity, from a classic paper by Cohen (1999: 58-9):

Mary and John are at the L.A. airport contemplating taking a certain flight to New York. They want to know whether the flight has a layover in Chicago. They overhear someone ask a passenger Smith if he knows whether the flight stops in Chicago. Smith looks at the flight itinerary he got from the travel agent and responds, 'Yes I know—it does stop in Chicago.' It turns out that Mary and John have a very important business contact to make at the Chicago airport. Mary says, 'How reliable is that itinerary? It could contain a misprint. They could have changed the schedule at the last minute.' Mary and John agree that Smith doesn't really know that the plane will stop in Chicago. They decide to check with the airline agent.... [N]either standard is simply correct or simply incorrect. Rather, context determines which standard is correct. Since the standards for knowledge ascriptions can vary across context, each claim, Smith's as well as Mary and John's, can be correct in the context in which it was made. When Smith says 'I know...', what he says is true given the weaker standard operating in that context. When Mary and John say 'Smith does not know...', what they say is true given the stricter standard operating in their context. *And there is no context independent correct standard.* (Emphasis in original.)

The pattern is the same as in the previous cases. There is, pre-theoretically, variability in what is said between contexts of utterance. As a result, the truth values can vary. In one context of speech, it is true to say Smith knows that the flight stops in Chicago, while in another (John and Mary's context), that very same sentence is not true. According to Cohen, this is because what he calls 'standards of knowledge' vary between contexts—standards can go up and down, and evidence that suffices in one context will not suffice in another. What you know depends on the standards in effect in the context you are in.

How can the context sensitivity of 'know' help respond to a skeptic who says we know nothing? The basic idea is this: the skeptical arguments such as those in Descartes' *Meditations* rely on putting you in a peculiar context by raising very strange and farfetched possibilities of error. The skeptic points out that you cannot rule out that you are dreaming or that you are a brain in a vat being fed all the perceptual inputs you currently think you are getting from reading this book. Note that if 'standards of knowledge' vary between contexts, there might be non-philosophical contexts in which the farfetched skeptical possibilities don't need to be ruled out. Maybe in some context, the standards for justification are 'lower' and so we don't need to rule out every bizarre potential source of error to count as knowing. On the other hand, maybe what happens in a philosophical context, e.g. when we talk about skepticism, is that standards of knowledge go 'up'. More sources of error need to be ruled out, and so knowing becomes more difficult. According to this view, the skeptic is right in a philosophical (high-standard) context, but wrong in an ordinary (low-standard) setting. The skeptic, so to speak, creates a context in which knowledge evaporates. (We return to the question of how what we say creates the context we are in in Chapter 11.)

1.3 Radical Contextualism: The View that Every Word is Context Sensitive

Reading the examples above, you might start to suspect that the phenomenon of context sensitivity is so ubiquitous that what is hard is not finding examples of context sensitivity, but finding counter-examples. Might it be that every word is context sensitive? Many philosophers think the answer is 'yes'. We call them *Radical Contextualists*. These passages from Travis (1996) and Searle (1980) can be seen as endorsement of that view:

What words mean plays a role in fixing when they would be true; but not an exhaustive one. Meaning leaves room for variation in truth conditions from one speaking to another. (Travis 1996: 451)

The literal meaning of a sentence only determines a set of truth conditions given a set of background practices and assumptions. Relative to one set of practices and assumption, a sentence may determine one set of truth conditions; relative to another set of practices and assumptions, another set; and if some sets of assumptions and practices are given, the literal meaning of a sentence may not determine a definite set of truth conditions at all. (Searle 1980: 227)

These are ambitious claims. There are many words. To have evidence for the conclusion that *all* of them are context sensitive, we need either a general argument to the effect that they *must* be or inductive evidence from a wide range of cases, which all turn out to be context sensitive. So far we have looked at just a few cases. The English language alone contains many thousands of words, so our sample is relatively minute.

In this chapter, we will not further pursue the question of how many words exhibit context sensitivity of the kind described above. We will simply note that there is fairly broad consensus among theorists working on this topic since the 1980s that a very large number of terms can make varied contributions to what is said—what there is disagreement about is how to classify that variability, an issue we address in Chapter 3.

1.3.1 On the philosophical significance of context sensitivity

This chapter has focused on making vivid the range of context sensitivity in language. One reaction to this might be: okay, there seems to be a lot of it. But why should philosophers care? What's the philosophical interest of this? Here are two answers to that question:

i. Intrinsic significance: It is one of the most intrinsically interesting questions that philosophers have worked on over the last 100 years. The various ways in which thought and talk interact with context are very hard to understand and philosophers have done some of the most groundbreaking work on that topic.
Here are two ways to make the challenge vivid:
- Suppose you were to build a robot that could interpret utterances the way we do. What would that robot have to be like? What kind of information about its surroundings would it need and what would it need to do with that information?
- Suppose you started out thinking of language mastery in the following naive way: *learning a language is to learn the meaning of the words and the grammatical rules. With that knowledge in hand you will be able to interpret any sentence that comes your way: your knowledge will enable you to understand what the speaker said (and wanted to communicate).* What this chapter has shown is that this picture is hopeless. What we know when we know how to interpret each other is more complex and in particular, it must include knowledge of the various ways in which context affects what we say to each other. How is that knowledge best systematized and described?

Work in philosophy and linguistics over the last 100 years has shown that answering these questions is among the most difficult challenges we humans have. Insofar as communication is at the center of human life, they are also central to understanding what it is to be a human being, i.e. central to our self-conception.

ii. Extrinsic significance: But not everyone enjoys thinking about the same kinds of questions. So for some the motivation for thinking philosophically about context sensitivity will have to be at least in part extrinsic. And there are plenty of reasons to care about context sensitivity, even if you don't find it intrinsically interesting. Here are two such reasons:
- First, as we have emphasized throughout the chapter: by understanding the context sensitivity of 'love', 'friendship', 'knowledge', etc., we learn something important about love, friendship, knowledge, etc. We learn that there isn't just one thing that is *love*, but a different thing for each context. That, if true, is in itself an important discovery for anyone interested in love. So, more generally, if there is some phenomenon, P, you are interested in, you should take an interest in whether 'P' is context sensitive, since it will tell you something important about P. If Radical Contextualism is true, then no matter what you are interested in—i.e. no matter what P is for you—questions about context sensitivity should matter to you.
- Second, as some of the cases above make clear, a proper understanding of context sensitivity can have very significant practical, non-philosophical, implications. The legal cases are sufficient to make that clear. To assess the legitimacy of the kind of ruling we cited there, we need to understand what counts as correct interpretation relative to a context. Or consider the slick Teflon politician who evades any missteps by appealing to context. She might always say things like 'you took my words out of context', but there are limits to when she can legitimately say that. The goal of this book is to provide a theoretical framework for understanding those limits.

1.3.2 *Varieties of context sensitivity—a taxonomy?*

So far we have talked about the kinds of context sensitivity above as if they were all of the same kind—or, at least, we haven't emphasized the differences between them. In the following chapters we will talk about the differences, but it is helpful here to highlight two important distinctions:

First Distinction: *Transparent vs nontransparent context sensitivity*: If we compare 'I' and 'now' on the one hand, and 'love', 'knowledge', and 'might' on the other, one salient difference is that the former pair wears their context sensitivity on their sleeves, so to speak, while the second pair does not. It's fairly easy to articulate a rule that specifies what 'I' or 'now', relative to any context, refers to. For example, relative to any context, 'I' refers to the speaker in the context. A little thought should reveal that this isn't the case with 'love': we can't articulate an informative rule that will give us what 'love' stands for in any context. The same is true of 'knows'. In this respect, 'loves' and 'knows' are importantly different from 'I' and 'now'.

Second Distinction: *Pure vs impure (or automatic vs discretionary)*: Secondly, it is worth noting that Kaplan (1977/1989) and Perry (2001), and many others following them, have emphasized a distinction between context-sensitive expressions like 'I' and 'now', on the one hand, and context-sensitive expressions like 'that' and 'it', on the other. Kaplan (1989: 490–1) calls this distinction the *pure/impure* indexical distinction; Perry (2001: 58–9) distinguishes between *automatic* and *discretionary* indexicals. We can separate out three points of difference characterizing this distinction.

- Automaticity: With impure indexicals, there is typically some question about what they are picking out in context. When Alex says "That's where I left my keys," she might be speaking in a moment of realization. Then, the audience could be left quite uncertain what she means by 'that'. Or she might be gesturing vaguely, narrowing down the candidates some but not fully. With pure indexicals, on the other hand, the context fully settles what is picked out. Once you know the context, you know exactly what the referent of 'I' or 'now' is.
- Self-Sufficiency: Impure indexicals are often accompanied by additional cues, such as pointings, which help settle their referent in context. Pure indexicals, on the other hand, do not typically come with such additional cues.
- Inevitability: Pure indexicals always get a referent in a context while impure indexicals do not. If Alex hallucinates a pink elephant, and tries to point and say, "That isn't normally there," her demonstrative fails to pick out anything. On the other hand, no matter how badly unmoored from her surroundings Alex becomes, her use of 'now' always picks out a time (the time of her utterance).

Observation #1.3 *More on the Automatic—Non-Automatic Distinction*

It is widely assumed in the literature that the distinction between automatic and non-automatic is a useful one. However, there is some doubt about how clear the distinction is. Consider, for example, the case of the political sloganeer.

> *Political Sloganeer: Charles is a member of Senator Jones' re-election campaign staff. Charles has been put in charge of designing and purchasing a number of billboards for the campaign. He creates a draft design with a picture of Senator Jones (a former star athlete in college) in a boxing ring, with the words "I'm fighting for your family's future" across the bottom. He then sends the design to Acme Billboards, where the design is implemented as a .jpg by software engineer Sam, and then sent to the printer, where printer Peter produces the full-size printout. Then Gus takes the printouts to the actual billboards and glues them up. A final billboard contains an occurrence/utterance of "I'm fighting for your future".*

The referent of the word 'I' on this billboard is Senator Jones, but there is no straightforward and automatic route from the utterance to the selection of a context that has Jones in the 'speaker' position—all of Charles, Sam, Peter, and Gus are also plausible candidates for standing in the appropriate relation to the utterance.

A similar case can call inevitability into question even for 'I'.

> *Fictional Candidate: Suppose now that there is no Senator Jones. Various shady business interests are putting together a campaign for a fictional candidate to split the opposition vote. Charles works for the campaign, but is unaware that there is no actual candidate. Then 'I' in his slogan 'I'm fighting for your future' doesn't refer to anything, in the same way that a demonstrative directed at a hallucination doesn't refer to anything.*

A final thought about traditional classifications: Self-sufficiency also doesn't seem to draw a sharp distinction between different indexicals. Demonstratives are often used without accompanying cues, as can be seen from the fact that they're used in written as well as spoken language. And cases that Kaplan regards as pure indexicals do often have accompanying cues. A pointing can identify one particular member of the audience as the referent of 'you'. Gestures may help indicate whether 'here' picks out this office, this building, this town, or this country. Even 'I' can be clarified by accompanying cues. Imagine the audience member who says into a portable microphone 'I have a question', while waving his arm to make it clear to the panel on stage who is speaking.

1.3.3 *Some burning questions*

We end this chapter with some salient and important questions that should be asked about the material just presented. Some of these issues will be addressed later in this book, while other issues must be pursued by reading external sources indicated in the text below.

1. WHAT ARE CONTEXTS AND HOW DO THEY SHAPE WHAT WE SAY?

We have presented some data to the effect that what is said by utterances can be sensitive to the context of utterance. Contexts of utterance, we've said, can determine what is picked out by 'love', 'knowledge', 'friend', 'use a firearm', 'now', 'might', and so on. We take that variability to be data that provides a starting point for theorizing about these issues. That data raises a number of very difficult questions, questions for which there's no pre-theoretic response. Below is a list of some important questions about contexts, and where in this book you can find discussion of those issues.

- How does a context determine what is picked out by a word? (See Chapters 4, 5, 6, and 7.)
- What kinds of things must contexts be to do what they seem to be doing? Is there just one kind of context or many? (See Chapters 5, 6, 7, and 8.)
- How do you as a speaker create and affect the context you are in? (See Chapters 8 and 9.)
- Do we have cognitive access to the relevant contextual features? Do we know or can we know what context we are in? (See Chapters 8 and 9.)

2. 'WHAT IS SAID': WHAT KIND OF THING IS THAT?

Throughout this chapter we talk about 'what is said'. What is that? In other words, what kind of things are sayings? That's a version of a question that has been at the center of much philosophical discussion for (at least) the last 100 years. It is a version of the question: how does language manage to represent the world? How can sounds, ink marks, and lights on a computer screen *say* something true or false, interesting, funny, important, or boring about the world? Is this ability of language to represent derivative of our ability to think about the world? If so, what is the connection between our thinking and linguistic meaning?

This book does not aim to provide an introduction to these questions and most of what we say below will remain neutral on the answer (although we'll say a bit about the question in Chapters 6 and 7).

CENTRAL POINTS IN CHAPTER 1

- The most obvious and non-controversial instances of linguistic context sensitivity are found in expressions in the Basic Set. The Basic Set includes expressions like 'I', 'here', 'now', and 'that'.
- These expressions exhibit three kinds of contextual variability: (i) What they refer to differs between contexts. (ii) What is said by sentences containing those expressions varies between contexts. (iii) The truth value of a sentence containing those expressions can vary between contexts.
- A large set of expressions outside the Basic Set also exhibit this kind of variability. Examples include 'love', 'friend', 'caused', 'might', and 'good'.
- Radical Contextualists are those who think *all* words are context sensitive.
- The set of context-sensitive expressions is not unified. They fall into various categories: transparent vs nontransparent, pure vs impure (though we have seen some reason for doubting the usefulness of those distinctions).

QUESTIONS FOR CHAPTER 1

Comprehension Questions

1.1. The truth value of an utterance containing 'I' depends on three things: what words are used in it, who says it, and how the world is. Describe scenarios that illustrate:
   a) Two utterances of stable form that say different things and have the same truth value
   b) Two utterances of stable form that say different things and have different truth values
   c) Two utterances of stable form that say the same thing and have the same truth value
1.2. The reference of 'I' is determined by a rule like the following:
   - Any utterance of 'I' refers to the speaker of that utterance.
   Give a similar such rule for 'tomorrow'.
1.3. Can you think of any other expressions that belong in the Basic Set of context-sensitive expressions?

1.4. Milly and Molly invent their own version of English in which 'dog' means cat. Is 'dog' then context sensitive? After all, in a context with Josh and Herman, 'dog' refers to dogs, while in any context with Milly and Molly it refers to cats.

Exploratory Questions

1.5. First consider the following sentences:
   (1) 'I bought a newspaper today.'
   (2) 'I own two newspapers.'
   (3) 'I work for a newspaper.'
   (4) 'Josh and I bought the same newspaper.'
   (5) 'I used a newspaper to keep the door open.'
   What are the different interpretations of 'newspaper' in these sentences? Should we think of 'newspaper' as ambiguous, context sensitive, both, or neither?
1.6. Next consider 'Smith' used as a surname. Is 'Smith' context sensitive or ambiguous? Does what we say in the text above help resolve this question?
1.7. In discussing love on p. 13, we said 'note that if "love" is context sensitive, then, in some important sense, what love is is also context sensitive. After all, love is the thing that the word "love" picks out.' Can the same point be extended to the context-sensitive words 'I' and 'now'? If not, why not?
1.8. Construct contexts of utterance for the sentence: 'Sally's put forward an interesting argument' where 'interesting' is interpreted in different ways.
1.9. Below is the headline and first paragraph of an article that was published in *The Onion* (http://www.theonion.com/blogpost/if-the-founding-fathers-were-alive-today-theyd-be-36620):

> If The Founding Fathers Were Alive Today, They'd Be Too Fascinated By A Garbage Disposal To Do Anything
>
> Nowadays, it seems like our country is more divided than ever. It's tougher and tougher to find something all Americans can agree on, and amid all this acrimony and infighting, one can't help but wonder if our nation's best days are behind us. In times like these, it only makes sense that we turn to the wisdom of the Founding Fathers, who, if they were alive today, would be too fascinated by a garbage disposal to do pretty much anything.

What are we keeping fixed and what have we updated (on analogy with the Caesar example) to get the intended interpretation of the title of this article?
1.10. Think of another case that illustrates the context sensitivity of causation.

1.11. David Lewis (1987: 183) says:

> For instance, suppose I write a strong recommendation that lands someone a job; so someone else misses out on that job and takes another; which displaces a third job-seeker; this third job-seeker goes elsewhere, and there meets and marries someone; their offspring and all their descendants forevermore would never have lived at all, and a fortiori would never have died, and so presumably their deaths would not have occurred, but for my act. Maybe there is a time after which every death that occurs is one that would not have occurred but for my act. It would be strange to single out my act as the cause of all those deaths. But it is a cause of them, under my analysis and also according to our common usage. And still I deny that I have ever killed.

Is Lewis right that he hasn't killed? If the answer is 'yes', why?

1.12. Which of the following are epistemic 'might's?
   (1) Hitler might have invaded Ireland if there was anything of worth in it
   (2) Might I suggest you calm down?
   (3) Julius Caesar might have invaded Ireland—there's no conclusive evidence to suggest he did, but he was in the area at one point

1.13. Think of a Cohen airport-style case from your recent experience.

1.14. Construct context-shifting examples for 'is red' (see Bezuidenhout (2002)), 'dances', 'weighs 80kg', 'is a sailor', 'is a philosopher', 'is happy', 'is clean', 'is rational', 'is a logical consequence', 'is true'.

1.15. Is "2+2=4" subject to context-shifting arguments?

1.16. Can you articulate a rule for 'here' in light of the following?
   (1) The bullet went through here.
   (2) On Mars, it is warmer than here.
   (3) In the US, they have a President, but here we have a Queen.
   (4) [Pointing to a map]: The invasion force will land here.
   (5) Here is the problem with your argument: you are assuming that reductivism is false.
   (6) [As the waiter hands the drink to the customer]: Here you are.

FURTHER READING FOR CHAPTER 1

For further readings on the Basic Set, and ways to diagnose context sensitivity, see Braun (2015), Cappelen and Lepore (2005) ch. 7, and Heim ('Lecture Notes On Indexicals', unpublished, section 5).

For further reading on gradable adjectives, see Kennedy (1997).

For further reading on 'might', see von Fintel and Gillies (2007), Kratzer (2012), and Egan and Weatherson (2011).

For further readings on counterfactual conditionals, see Edgington (2005), Bennett (2003), ch. 10.

For further reading on causation, see Schaffer (2012) and Paul and Hall (2013).

For further reading on knowledge, see Rysiew (2011) and Lewis (1996).

For further reading on Radical Contextualism, see Sperber and Wilson (1986), Travis (1996), Carston (2002), Recanati (2001, 2004), Cappelen and Lepore (2005).

For replies, consult Leslie (2007), Hawthorne (2006), Cappelen and Hawthorne (2009), and Sennet and Lepore (2010).

For interesting variations on cases of context sensitivity that cause problems for our attempted taxonomy, see Predelli (1998), Egan (2009).

For discussions about the metaphysical nature of what is said, see McGrath (2012), and King, Soames, and Speaks (2014).

2

Stability Across Contexts

2.1 Where We Are and the Plan for This Chapter

The previous chapter presented some powerful evidence that what is said by sentences, and hence their truth values can vary between contexts of utterance: the same sentence can be true when uttered in one context, and false when uttered in another.

The goal of this chapter is to introduce you to a seemingly essential feature of language that, at least at first glance, appears to be in tension with the data we laid out in the first chapter.

It seems essential to language that the meaning of a word be stable across contexts. It is hard to see how language can perform the functions it in fact does unless there is a fundamental form of stability in what-is-said by utterances of sentences (i.e. unless what is said does *not* vary between contexts). The goal of this chapter is to present this stability data and the goal of the next chapter is to present ways of resolving the tension between variability and stability.

2.2 Three Arguments for Stability

In what follows we outline three kinds of data that appear to show that what our sentences say does not vary between contexts. The three kinds of data are:

i. Gathering, transmitting, and using information require contextual stability.
ii. The way we say what other people have said requires stability across contexts.

iii. The way interpretation seems to us 'from the inside' requires contextual stability.

We consider each of these in turn.

2.2.1 Stability 1: the cognitive and communicative role of what is said requires stability across contexts

The first chapter of this book presented lots of data and examples. It didn't contain a lot of arguments. Most of philosophy, however, consists of argumentation. And so what we now outline is an argument of the form: here is something we do with language. For language to work that way, what is said has to be stable between contexts. The conclusion of this argument is that extensive context sensitivity is incompatible with the role of what is said in gathering, transmitting, and using the information we get from people we talk to. Since language is a tool we have created for sharing and storing information, we can assume it isn't massively context sensitive since this would undermine its purpose.

The argument goes like this. Suppose someone tells you something by uttering a sentence, say, 'Samantha, who is very smart, loves her friend Alex'. The utterance takes place in a particular context (i.e. at a certain place, to a certain audience, as part of a certain conversation, etc.)—call this *the Original Context*. To make things vivid, suppose that this information is very important to you. Since what you were told is important to you, you want to remember it. You need to be able to store and recall that information for later use. For example, this information can play a role in your reasoning about what to *do* later (for example, because she's very smart, you might ask Samantha for help with a project you're working on). Since you are a social creature, you will also want to *tell* others what you have been told. The central point in the argument we're now sketching is that widespread context sensitivity makes these roles for what is said difficult, if not impossible to fulfill.

Here is why: If the data from Chapter 1 is correct, then what is said by uttering a sentence in a context is massively influenced by the specific features of that context. There are many contexts and so a large number of different things the sentence could say. With that in mind, consider some options for how to preserve in memory the information you got from the original utterance.

Option 1: You could store the fact that you heard the sentence in memory.

Problem with Option 1: If you were to recall the sentence 'Samantha, who is very smart, loves her friend Alex' in another context, what it says in that new context could be very different from what it said in the Original Context. Recall from Chapter 1: 'smart', 'love', and 'friend' can vary in what they mean between contexts. In the new context, those words could mean different things. So by recalling the sentence in the new context you fail to recall the same information.

The same concern arises if you want to tell someone else what you have been told. If what you have remembered is the sentence 'Samantha, who is very smart, loves her friend Alex', then by uttering the sentence to them in the new context, you will likely mislead. In the new context, the words in that sentence can mean different things from what they meant in the original context. As a result, what you tell them by uttering the sentence in the new context isn't what you were told. The context has changed and so what you say by uttering that sentence is different.

In sum: If the data in Chapter 1 is correct, then to retain and transmit the information you were told, you can't *just* remember the sentence.

Option 2: You could try to remember not just the sentence but also all the relevant features of the Original Context, or at least all those features that determine the meaning of e.g. 'love', 'smart', and 'friend'. If so, then you could try one of two strategies to ensure stability in what is said:

(i) You could make sure to place yourself in a context that's sufficiently similar to the Original Context and then recall the sentence,
(ii) You could try to find a new sentence that in the new context says what 'Samantha, who is very smart, loves her friend Alex' said in the original context.

Problems with Option 2: The basic problem with this option is simply that we have no idea how to do it. We just don't know what the relevant features of contexts are. In simple cases, like 'I', 'here', and 'now', we have a pretty clear idea (it is the speaker, location, and time of the original context), but in slightly more complex cases we're pretty much in the dark. Not even theorists who have worked on this over a lifetime claim to have a clear idea of what the relevant contextual features are for words like 'love', 'friend', 'smart', etc. Since this option would place impossible demands on us, it can't be right.

Option 3: Suppose in the Original Context you didn't store the sentence in memory, but instead a sentence that *in some context-insensitive way preserved the same information*. Then, it would seem, the problems with the first two options disappear. We would then be able to preserve the information we have been told, despite the kind of massive context sensitivity outlined in Chapter 1.

Problems with Option 3: Arguably, there is no such sentence. Recall from Chapter 1 philosophers like Searle and Travis who think there are no sentences that don't exhibit context sensitivity. They think the kind of variability we appealed to in our examples in Chapter 1 can be found for *any* sentence. Of course, Chapter 1 didn't show that the Radical Contextualists are right. But even if they are wrong, they have shown that it isn't easy to find sentences that aren't amenable to context-shifting arguments. So even in the cases where there is such a sentence, formulating it would be extraordinarily difficult. Moreover, even if we *could* do it, it is fairly clear that we as a matter of fact *don't do it*. To illustrate the above points, consider again the sentence 'Samantha, who is very smart, loves her friend Alex'. First, there might be no sentence in English that expresses, in a context-insensitive way, exactly what this sentence expresses in its context of utterance. Second, even if there is such a sentence, none of us know what that sentence is. Third, we don't, as a matter of fact, make the effort to remember such sentences—if we did, we would be aware that we do, and we are not.

Here is a tentative summary of the above line of thought: A central function of language is to store and transmit information. That role cannot be easily performed by a language that is massively context sensitive. Of course, it doesn't logically follow that context-sensitive expressions are not ubiquitous in language. Maybe our language just performs these functions poorly, or maybe we have mischaracterized the function. Both those options will be explored below. What we want to emphasize at this point is simply that there is a prima facie tension between the need for cross-contextual stability, on the one hand, and cross-contextual variability of the kind described in Chapter 1 on the other.

2.2.2 Stability 2: saying what others said: the simple way and the hard way

Imagine Jill uttering the sentence 'In St Andrews, you can see the impressive ruins of a huge cathedral which took about 150 years to complete and was consecrated on July 5, 1318' while standing on Market Street at 1pm on July 1, 2015. Call that the Original Context. Now, we don't know you, reader, but whoever you are, ask yourself how you would report what Jill said. We expect that one answer you will come up with is the following:

> *The Report:* Jill said that in St Andrews you can see the impressive ruins of a huge cathedral which took about 150 years to complete and was consecrated on July 5, 1318.

This is a great way of saying what Jill said, *no matter what context you are in*. The Report can be used to say what Jill said in any context. It doesn't matter where you are, who you are, or what you are talking about, you can still use The Report to say what Jill said.

Here is why that's important: note that in The Report, the words after 'Jill said that' are exactly the same words as Jill used in the Original Context. So we are using the same words as she used to say the same thing that she said. And we can do that in any context. But then it looks like those words must say the same in every context (because in every context they can be used to say what she said). But then those words can't vary in meaning between contexts (because if they did, they couldn't be used to say the same in each context).

In sum: the ease with which we use Jill's very words to say what she said is evidence against the kind of massive context sensitivity we outlined in the first chapter. This of course wouldn't be very interesting if it were a very restricted phenomenon. But it is not. Take the non-basic cases of context sensitivity from the previous chapter. They can—in a wide range of cases—be reported in the same simple way (i.e. by using the very same words). To help you see that, consider the following utterances, also by Jill (and also in the Original Context):

1. Naomi loves Alex.
2. If Caesar had been in command, he would have used catapults.
3. Naomi knows flight KL407 stops in Chicago.
4. Drought caused the great Indian famine.

Now ask yourself how you would report what Jill said in your context. We predict that 1*–4* would be great answers:

1*. Jill said that Naomi loves Alex.
2*. Jill said that if Caesar had been in command, he would have used catapults.
3*. Jill said that Naomi knows that the flight stops in Chicago.
4*. Jill said that drought caused the great Indian famine.

Those reports are true. If so, what comes after 'said that' in each of the reports must say the same thing as what the original sentence said in the Original Context. If so, you've been able to say what Jill said using her very words, but in a very different context from the one in which Jill originally spoke. So, it seems, what is said by sentences 1–4 should be the same across contexts.

The case against widespread context sensitivity can be strengthened as follows: There is a subclass of expressions, those we called the *Basic Set* in Chapter 1, where simple saying-reports of the kind considered above are blocked. Suppose Jill utters 'I am happy' or 'I am here now' or 'I had fish for dinner yesterday'. Suppose you are tasked with saying what Jill said. How would you do it? Note that you cannot do it the simple way by just using her words to say what she said. If you tried any of these, you would fail:

- Jill said that I am happy.
- Jill said that I am here now.
- Jill said that I had fish for dinner yesterday.

Jill didn't talk about you, your time, or your place. To report correctly, you have to make adjustments. You would have to take away the word from the basic set and replace them with ones that in your context mean what her words meant in her context. You could try 'Jill said that Jill was happy' or 'Jill said that Jill was happy there and then' or 'Jill said that Jill had fish for dinner on Thursday' (assuming the original speech took place on Friday). The argument continues: *This is exactly as expected if a word is context sensitive. Context sensitivity implies that you have to adjust and coordinate meanings between contexts.* So we can conclude: these are the genuinely context-sensitive expressions. The others are not context sensitive. So, contrary to what we said in Chapter 1, it now looks like context sensitivity is restricted to a very small subset of expressions, namely to the ones we called the Basic Set in Chapter 1.

> **Observation #2.1** *The Difference Between Direct and Indirect Reports*
>
> Above we said that if Jill utters 'I am happy', Josh could not say what she said by uttering:
>
> - Jill said that I am happy.
>
> If he uttered that sentence, he would have said that Jill said that Josh is happy, but she did not say that (she was talking about herself, not about Josh). However, what Josh could have said is:
>
> - Jill said, 'I am happy'.
>
> This latter report is called 'a direct quotation' of what Jill said, the former an 'indirect quotation'. In the direct quotation we simply report on the words used. In the indirect quotation, we use our words to say what Jill said. One way to see the difference is to note that Herman, who is Norwegian, could have correctly indirectly reported Jill by saying:
>
> - Jill sa at hun var glad.
>
> i.e., by using Norwegian words to say what Jill said (even though Jill might not understand Norwegian). Herman could not, however, report Jill with the Norwegian direct report:
>
> - Jill sa, 'Jill var glad'.
>
> If he said that, he would have said that Jill spoke Norwegian.

2.2.3 Stability 3: ease of cross-contextual understanding

The previous section focused on how we report what people say. The phenomenon of simple speech reports (those that re-use the words the speaker used) provides evidence of stability of content. There is a correlate of this in our sense of understanding each other—call this the 'experience or phenomenology of understanding'. Imagine now encountering 5–8 in a book or on a recording:

5. Naomi loves Alex.
6. If Caesar had been in command, he would have used catapults.
7. Naomi knows flight KL407 stops in Chicago.
8. Drought caused the great Indian famine.

Here is a hypothesis: It is easy for you, no matter what context you are located in, to understand these speech events. Of course, one way to show this is to point out that you can easily say what the speaker said (i.e. use a simple speech report). But focus now not on how you would verbally report what was said. Focus, instead, on the immediacy of understanding. This is, admittedly, a bit elusive, but is nonetheless a real phenomenon. Our informants, at least, report a striking difference between, on the one hand, their sense of immediately understanding 5–8, and on the other their lack of understanding of 9–11 (when the context of utterance is unknown):

9. Yesterday she went there.
10. That hit that.
11. It's on top of it.

If you encounter sentences 9–11 without knowing what was demonstrated, what day it was uttered, what the location was, etc., there would be a very salient sense in which you had no idea what the speaker said.

Again, this argument is supposed to draw your attention to a very striking difference between cases of context-sensitive expressions from the Basic Set (such as 'yesterday', 'that', and 'she') on the one hand, and expressions such as 'knows', 'caused', and 'loves' on the other.

CENTRAL POINTS IN CHAPTER 2

The overall sense after reading this chapter should be that the picture we have from Chapter 1 is at best incomplete. While there's some evidence that what we say using one and the same sentence varies widely between contexts, there are also good reasons to think that our sentences have an important kind of stability. This was brought out in three ways: (1) Stability is what guarantees that we can retain, transmit, and use information across contexts. (2) Stability is revealed by how easy it is to say what others said (we can, often, just use the very same words they used—even if we are in a different context). (3) We often grasp what was said in a different context with a kind of immediacy that would be surprising if language was massively context sensitive.

> QUESTIONS FOR CHAPTER 2

Comprehension Questions

2.1. Describe two contexts that illustrate the problem with Option 1 above.
2.2. Having done so, try to find a context-invariant way of saying what your sentence said in the original context you described.
2.3. What is the difference between the sentences 'Jill said 'I am here now'' and 'Jill said that I am here now'?

Exploratory Questions

2.4. Why is it important to store information in memory? Does it matter if what you store in memory changes a bit every time you recall it?
2.5. Consider the following case:

> Jill says, 'Stone floats', speaking in a context in which what matters is whether things float on liquid mercury. We're now on a sinking ship, looking for a way to make our getaway and avoid landing in the shark-infested waters. I suggest using a slab of stone as a raft. You say that that's ridiculous, and I say, 'Don't worry, Jill said that stone floats'.

Is this true? If the answer is 'no', what does that tell us about the 'easiness' of simple speech reports?

2.6. Can you construct a case where we cannot use a simple speech report of an utterance of 'Josh is fast'? I.e. first describe a context for an utterance of 'Josh is fast' by a speaker S. Then a different context, in which 'S said that Josh is fast' is false. Use the 'Stone floats' example as a model.

> FURTHER READING FOR CHAPTER 2

For more on the first argument for stability, see Cappelen and Lepore (2005), Hawthorne (2006), and Timothy Williamson 2005).

3

Some Strategies for Reconciling Stability and Variability

3.1 Where We Are and the Plan for This Chapter

How do we reconcile the variability data outlined in Chapter 1 and the stability data in Chapter 2? We are faced with a dilemma:

On the one hand, what we say to each other by uttering sentences is shaped in all kinds of interesting ways by the context we are in when we speak. We are going to assume, in what follows, that the context sensitivity of what is said is wide-ranging along two dimensions: many words are context-sensitive and the range of potential meanings is wide. Moreover, what is said by an utterance is sensitive to features of context that are non-transparent to us: speakers and audiences have no easy cognitive access to the contextual mechanisms that shape what we say.

On the other hand, what we say in uttering a sentence in a given context can easily be grasped and said again in a different context. We tell others what someone told us, repeat a point we've made before, discuss the same question over and over again, remember what we were told—in all these cases we say (or think) the same thing in different contexts. If someone says to us, 'There are many naked mole rats in Sweden and their behavior is very interesting', then we can easily tell this to other people. We can, for example, say to you, our reader:

- There are many naked mole rats in Sweden and their behavior is very interesting.

We are confident that we just told you, reader, no matter what context you are in, is the same as what we were told.

The underlying puzzle is this: how do we reconcile variability and stability? If what we say is fixed in all kinds of ways by our speech contexts, how can what we say be so easily transferred *across* contexts? We know of no complete solution to this problem, but we will explore some strategies for reconciliation that have been influential in the recent literature. The solutions divide into three broad categories:

(i) An appeal to similarity: This strategy in effect denies the data in Chapter 2 (or reinterprets it), and concludes that the puzzle is resolved in that way.

(ii) An appeal to contextual parasites: This strategy introduces the idea of a 'contextual parasite' and uses that to account for the data in Chapter 2. The basic idea is this: What Chapter 2 took to be communication across contexts isn't. Parasites have the effect of making context-sharing easier than we thought and so make same-saying easier than we thought.

(iii) An appeal to pluralistic minimalism: This strategy aims to reconcile the stability data in Chapter 2 and the variability data in Chapter 1. The basic strategy is to appeal to two ideas: in uttering a sentence, you say many things, some of these vary between contexts while some of them are stable. So we have variability and stability. This strategy comes in several varieties, depending on what the stable— minimal—what is said is taken to be.

As with the rest of this book, the classification of views is not exhaustive—they are but one way to structure a vast and complex debate that has gone on for more than fifty years. The aim is not exhaustiveness, but rather to provide a way into a complex topic. If you are able to understand and think through the arguments in the remainder of this chapter, you will most certainly be in a good position to engage with the remaining literature on the topic.

3.2 First Strategy for Resolving the Puzzle: Stability is an Illusion and We Can Expect No More Than Similarity

Chapter 2 sketched an argument to the effect that widespread context sensitivity is incompatible with the preservation of what-was-said in memory and the transfer of information to others. In response, the friends of widespread context sensitivity can say the following:

Suppose Jill tells me something by uttering:

- Samantha, who is very smart, loves her friend Alex.

According to friends of this strategy, it is true that I can't recall exactly what Jill said, or say exactly what she said in another context. Typically, the best I can do is re-express and recall something similar. But that is fine—life goes on even if we don't have the very same information preserved between contexts. As long as what we preserve is similar enough for practical purposes, there is no reason for concern. As long as the standards for 'smart', 'love', and 'friend' are not massively off, communication is smooth.

Here is a passage from Anne Bezuidenhout (2002) that expresses a view of this kind:

Since utterance interpretation is always in the first place colored by one's own cognitive perspective, I think we should reject the idea that there is an intermediate stage in communication which involves the recovery of some content shared by speaker and listener and which is attributed by the listener to the utterance. In communication... [w]e need recognize only speaker-relative utterance content and listener-relative utterance content and a relation of similarity holding between these two contents.... This does not mean that we have to deny that lateral interpretation requires the preservation of something. But this something need simply be a relevant degree of similarity between the thought expressed by the speaker and the thought expressed by the listener. (Bezuidenhout 2002: 212–13)

Likewise, Sperber and Wilson (1995) write:

It seems to us neither paradoxical nor counterintuitive to say that there are thoughts that we cannot exactly share, and that communication can be successful without resulting in an exact duplication of thoughts in communicator and audience. We see communication as a matter of enlarging mutual cognitive environments, not of duplicating thoughts. (Sperber and Wilson 1995: 192–3)

Here is a way to understand this view: Sentences like:

- A said that p
- A said what B said
- A understands what B said

and other such locutions do not require identity of what-was-said to be true. All they require is similarity. The details can be elucidated in various ways, one version of which is:

- 'A said that p' means the same as 'A said something similar to p.'
- 'A said what B said' means the same as 'A said something similar to what B said.'

This is a fairly widely endorsed response to the arguments in Chapter 2 and it provides an attractive strategy for defending widespread context sensitivity, e.g. the kind of radical contextualist mentioned in Chapter 1. We turn now to some criticism of this view. Our focus will be on a couple of objections from Cappelen and Lepore 2006.

Criticism 1: False predictions

Consider these two claims:

1: The US has forty-nine states.
2: The US has fifty states.

These claims are similar—or at least, relative to some contexts they are similar (after all, forty-nine is very close to fifty). Now recall that according to the Similarity Reply a report of the form 'Jill said that ...' is true if what goes in for '...' is sufficiently similar to what Jill said. Now imagine Jill saying: 'The US has fifty states'. Suppose John tries to report her by saying: 'Jill said that the US has forty-nine states'. Notice that this report is false. Jill didn't say that the US has forty-nine states, she said that the US has *fifty* states. There is no context in which it is true to say that Jill said that the US has forty-nine states. That's just wrong. This, the argument goes, shows that the Similarity Reply fails. The Similarity Reply predicts that 'Jill said that the US has forty-nine states' should be true as long as 'the US has forty-nine states' is sufficiently similar to 'The US has fifty states'. But we have just seen that this is wrong. In order to say what Jill said, you have to say that she said that the US has fifty states (note: not even saying that she said that the US has 49.9999999999 would do, even though that's even more similar to saying the US has fifty states).

Criticism 2: 'If A said the same as B and B said the same as C, then C said the same as A'

Suppose we tell you the following:

- A said the same as B and B said the same as C.

With that information in hand, you can infer that if A said that the US has fifty states, then that's what B said and also what C said, and so C said the same as A. (One way to put this is to say that 'said the same as' is a transitive relation, but you don't need to understand that terminology to understand the point below.) However, note that if we tell you the following:

- A is similar to B and B is similar to C

you should not infer that A is similar to C. If A is similar to B in one respect (e.g. how she walks) and B is similar to C in a very different respect (e.g. how she writes), it does not follow that A and C are similar (similarity is not transitive, to use the jargon above).

Again, we have evidence that 'said the same' is very different from 'is similar to'. This is reason to think that the strategy behind the Similarity Reply—to spell out 'said the same' in terms of 'is similar to'—must fail. The point in this section can be summed up as follows: sameness cannot be understood in terms of similarity and so same-saying cannot be understood in terms of similarity-saying.

3.3 Second Strategy for Resolving the Puzzle: Contextual Parasites Give Us Stability without Denying Radical Variability

The first strategy was an effort to deny or explain away the data in Chapter 2. We now consider a strategy that aims to reconcile that data with the complete endorsement of the data in Chapter 1. At the core of this strategy is an appeal to so-called 'contextual parasites'.

3.3.1 *Contextual parasites: an introduction*

To explain this strategy, we first have to say a bit about what 'contextual parasites' are. They are most easily introduced through an example. Suppose John utters 'I turned left just before a nearby bar.' Mia then reports John by saying, 'John said that he turned left just before a nearby bar.' Mia's utterance can be true despite her being in a location and with an orientation different from John's. How is that possible? Here is an answer that's potentially helpful to the contextualist: 'left' and 'nearby' end up meaning the same in Mia's mouth as they did in John's because those words in Mia's mouths are *parasitic* on John's utterance. By 'parasitic' we mean that they pick up their meaning from John's utterance: whatever he meant by them, Mia means by them. The meaning is inherited.

Here is an example from Lloyd Humberstone (2006, pp. 315–16) that illustrates parasitism of the kind we have in mind:

Suppose that a mother in England wants to warn her daughter that the street food in Bombay, which the daughter is about to visit, is unsafe. She can do so, while both are still in England and travel plans are under discussion, by saying:

(1) The local street food is not safe—please promise you'll stick to the hotel restaurant.

The daughter can write back after arrival:

(2) You were right—the local street food isn't safe, as I found to my cost last night.

And the mother can then report to others:

(3) My daughter confirmed that the local street food is indeed unsafe.

So the phrase 'the local street food' can be interpreted as 'the street food in the contextually salient location', where one way of making a location salient is by speaking (or writing from) there, but another is by reporting on what someone there has said: embedding this in indirect quotation does not hijack the salient location automatically to that of the reporter.

Humberstone in this passage emphasizes that the daughter's location is salient to the mother (she knows where the daughter is and that location is 'on her mind', so to speak), but it is important to note that this isn't required for parasitic reference to take place. The example works fine even if we change it so that the mother doesn't know *where* the daughter is (and so the location of the daughter is not salient to her). If the daughter travels around quite a bit, the mother can report 'My daughter told me that the local street food is unsafe', she can even add 'I'm not sure where she is, but I hope she heeds my warning'. The mother's use of 'local' picks up on the right location because it is parasitic on the original context of utterance.

Here is an analogy to see how contextual parasitism works. Consider the occurrences of 'she' and 'it' in the following sentence:

- Angelika bought a book, and then she lost it.

The meanings of both 'she' and 'it' depend on words earlier in the sentence: the meaning of 'she' is inherited from 'Angelika' and the meaning of 'it' depends on 'a book'. Here the inheritance takes place within a sentence. In the cases we considered above, the inheritance is not within a sentence. It happens across both sentences and contexts, but it might be that the basic phenomenon is the same (or at least closely related).

3.3.2 *Parasitism and the puzzle*

Here is an important point to note: What parasitism in effect does is *merge* contexts. Take an expression like 'rich'. Let's for simplicity say that a use of that expression will pick from the context of utterance a *standard for richness*—different contexts have different standards of richness associated with them (e.g., rich by the standards of a medieval peasant, rich by the standards of a Russian oligarch, etc.). When we report on an utterance containing 'rich' in another context and we do so parasitically, then the context of the report inherits the standard of richness from the original context of utterance.

Note the following:

i. Parasitism makes it easier to say what others have said by making features of contexts easier to share. When we say what someone said, we reach back into the original speech context, so to speak. We grab, for example, the standards of richness from that context and transfer it to our context.

ii. Note that so described the solution circumvents the puzzle as we described it at the beginning of this chapter. We described the puzzle in this way: how can we communicate across varied contexts, when what we say is shaped by context? Parasitism bypasses the problem: *it makes what is said stable by making it easy to merge contexts*. It is not a strategy that secures the same what is said across different contexts. It is, instead, a strategy that secures sameness of contexts, and so, as a corollary, sameness of what is said.

This helps those defending widespread context sensitivity. If *context-sharing* is as easy as parasitism makes it seem, then the problem for cross-contextual communication seems less urgent (because we have an easy strategy, parasitism, for merging contexts).

3.3.3 *Parasitism: four problems and some proposed solutions*

Parasitism is a promising strategy for resolving the puzzle, but it is not without problems. Here are four of them, with some proposed thoughts about possible solutions:

3.3.3.1 FIRST PROBLEM: PARASITISM DOESN'T ALWAYS WORK. WHY NOT?

Not all context-sensitive terms allow for parasitism. To see that, consider this case:

> Imagine Jill uttering 'I am happy'. Now imagine Sam trying to say what Jill said in a different context. He has read about parasitism, and so he tries to say what Jill said by uttering: 'Jill said that I am happy'. He's hoping his use of the context sensitive expression 'I' will be parasitic on Jill's utterance. But of course, that doesn't work. What Sam ends up saying is that he, Sam, is happy. And that is not what Jill said. There seems to be no way for him to get his use of 'I' to be parasitic on Jill's context (the context in which Jill is the speaker and so the referent to 'I').

The same seems to be true, for example, of 'now', 'here', 'you', and 'yesterday'. A challenge for the appeal to parasites is to explain why certain context-sensitive terms lend themselves to parasitism while others don't. Roughly, all the basic cases in Chapter 1 fail to be parasitic, while the rest (like 'know', 'might', 'friend', 'love' etc.) can be parasitic.

One response to this is to treat it as an observation: some context-sensitive terms can be parasitic, others cannot. Maybe we shouldn't worry about explaining why that is so. Maybe it is simply a basic fact about them—it is written into their meaning, so to speak. If our goal is to describe important facts about context sensitivity and use those to explain the puzzle, then it might suffice to mark the difference between the parasitical and the non-parasitical, and leave it at that.

3.3.3.2 SECOND PROBLEM: COLLECTIVE REPORTS

We sometimes report on multiple utterances at the same time. So imagine the following exchange:

- Jill (who is in Miami) utters: 'Naomi went to a nearby beach.'
- Nicole (who is in Oslo) utters: 'Naomi went to a nearby beach.'
- Amanda (who is in Hong Kong) utters: 'Jill and Nicole said that Naomi went to a nearby beach.'

How does 'nearby' in Amanda's utterance manage to say what both Jill and Nicole said? Jill used 'nearby' to mean 'near Miami', Nicole used 'nearby' to mean 'near Oslo', but somehow Amada managed to use 'nearby' to say what both Jill and Nicole said. Amanda simultaneously reports on two different utterances made in two different contexts. The report is still true. This is a problem for the appeal to parasitism if we assume that an expression can only be parasitic on one context at a time. If so, parasitism can't explain how Amanda's utterance manages to pick up on both Jill's and Nicole's utterances.

Some authors (e.g. Cappelen and Lepore 2005) take this to undermine the parasitism reply (and so to be an important argument against contextualists of various sorts). Others, such as Cappelen and Hawthorne, think the problem can be overcome by finding a non-parasitic account of how Amanda's report is true (see Cappelen and Hawthorne 2009, chapter 2).

3.3.3.3 THIRD PROBLEM: 'HOW DOES IT WORK?'

What exactly makes it the case that a particular utterance is parasitic on another one? How do the two utterances connect? Talk of parasites is a metaphor (there aren't real little parasites in our utterances)—to get a real explanation, we need to cash out the metaphor.

There is no standard answer to this and research on contextual parasites is still at an early stage. One option is that the reporter (the one who says what someone else says) *intends* for her words to be parasitic on another context/expression. There's an intention of the form, *this utterance of the expression 'rich' should mean the same as 'rich' meant when Jill said it* (where Jill is the original speaker).

However, it might not be a realistic assumption that the speaker always has a conscious or even subconscious intention of this form. For one thing, she might not remember what the original context was.

Suppose you remember being told that naked mole rats are very interesting, but you don't remember where and when you were told. One picture of parasites is that you are still connected to the original context of utterances—there is a chain of communication going from the original context of utterance to you. (A spoke to B, B spoke to C, C spoke to D, and then D told you.) So there's a chain of 'naked mole rats are very interesting'-utterances going back from you to A, even if you are unaware of it.) Maybe, again, the best we can do is resort to a metaphor. There's what we can call a communicative-contextual string (or chain) going between speakers and contexts. It is anchored in the original speech context and other contexts are connected to it through this communicative-contextual string. Of course, the metaphor of a 'communicative-contextual'-string will have to be cashed out at some point—and this is an area of future research.

This ends our discussion of the appeal to parasites. It strikes us as one of the most plausible strategies for resolving the puzzle of explaining the compatibility between the stability and variability of language. As we have just noted, there is work to be done here, but that is to be expected. This is an area of research that is still in its infancy.

3.4 Third Strategy for Resolving the Puzzle: Minimalistic Pluralism

We turn now to a third influential strategy for resolving the puzzle. The basic idea is to deny a tacit but fundamental assumption that generates the puzzle. The puzzle, as we articulated it, assumes that there is just one thing which is said by the utterance of a sentence. If we make that assumption, then it looks mysterious how we can have both variability and stability in what was said. Take a sentence like 'There are many naked mole rats in Sweden and their behavior is very interesting'. According to Chapter 1, that sentence can be used to say many different things in different contexts. According to Chapter 2, it is also important that what it says is stable across contexts (only then can we use it to preserve and transmit information).

But suppose that each time one utters the sentence, it says many different things. If so, then one of those can be stable across contexts while others may vary. Let's call the view that an utterance of a sentence says only one thing (that there is only one what is said per utterance per context, so to speak) *What Is Said Monism* (*Monism* for short). One salient option when faced with the problem outlined at the beginning of this chapter is to give up Monism. The alternative is some version of what we will call *What Is Said Pluralism* (*Pluralism* for short). Pluralism is the view that in each context many things are said by an utterance of a sentence. If Pluralism is true, we can easily reconcile the stability and variability data: one what is said is stable and then there is variability in the rest of what is said.

Structurally, the solution is clear enough, but it raises at least two tricky questions:

i. What is the stable element in all these cases? How do we pick it? How do we describe it?
ii. Do we have any positive reason to think Pluralism is true or is it simply an ad hoc move to solve the puzzle?

First some brief remarks in reply to 2, and then in the next section we will turn to 1.

3.4.1 Brief Explanation of What Is Said Pluralism

The primary evidence for Pluralism is independent of the puzzle. Consider the following case:

> Jones is under suspicion of the murder of Smith, and is being interrogated by the police. Eventually Jones says, 'I'm the one who killed Smith'. The police tell the press 'Jones said that he is the murderer', or 'Jones said that he is guilty', or 'Jones said that he committed the heinous crime'.

These are all correct reports of what Jones said. Moreover, if you know that Smith is a Swede, and if that is important and relevant in your context, you can report Jones as having said that he killed a Swede.

In short, the situation is this: Jones uttered the sentence 'I'm the one who killed Smith' and the following are all true reports of what he said:

- Jones said that he is the murderer
- Jones said that he is guilty
- Jones said that he committed the heinous crime
- Jones said that he killed the Swede

Since these are all true reports, it follows that Smith said many things (he said that he is the murder, that he is guilty, that he committed the heinous crime, that he killed the Swede).

There is nothing special about this particular case. In general, when someone utters a sentence there are many different true ways to say what he or she said. And so the point applies very generally: by uttering one sentence, a speaker says a plurality of things, not just one thing.

3.4.2 What is the Minimal What Is Said?

We turn now to the second challenge for minimalistic pluralism: what is the stable component of what is said? When minimalists say that one thing said is 'minimal', they mean to indicate *that context plays a minimal role in shaping it*. This is as expected if we want a what is said that is shared across contexts (if it was influenced by context, it would vary between contexts and so not have cross-contextual stability).

Consider utterances of 'Naomi is smart' in different contexts. What is said by such utterances will depend on the contextually supplied comparison class. In some contexts, it can be used to say she is smart for a kid in kindergarten. In others, it can be used to say that she is smart compared to rocket scientists. This is just a way of repeating the data from Chapter 1 with respect to 'smart'. Speech act pluralism allows the pluralistic-minimalist to grant this. We are now looking for what these utterances have in common and why it is we can, for example, share that content across contexts. According to minimalists, the simple answer is this: *that Naomi is smart*. That is what is invariant between contexts.

Two more examples to illustrate this strategy: We said that what counts as 'love' in a context depends on contextually shiftable standards. Loving an actor or a movie or a family member, might require standards different from what we often think of in cases involving romantic love. Now consider a series of utterances of 'Naomi loves Jill', in different contexts with different standards in play. One component of what is said will vary, but there's a stable element in all of them: *that Naomi loves Jill*. The minimal what is said attributes *love* without any relativization. This, according to the pluralistic minimalist, is the common element in the different utterances (that also say different things—according to the pluralistic component of the view).

Finally, consider another example much discussed in the literature: sentences containing 'ready'. Imagine a series of utterances of 'Jill is ready'. One such utterance says that Jill is ready to go to school, one that she is ready to play tennis, one that she is ready for a bath, etc. Despite this, any one of these utterances can be reported by 'X said that Jill is ready' (where X is the person who uttered the original sentence). So it looks like there's a common element—*that Jill is ready*—that somehow is said by all those different utterances of 'Jill is ready'.

The question many have had about minimalism is this: what is it for Naomi to be smart in the minimal sense? What is it for Naomi to love Jill in the minimal sense? What is it for Jill to be ready in the minimal sense? To see how puzzling these and related questions are, consider the following dialogue:

A: Alice is ready.
B: Okay, what is she ready for? For going to bed or for her exam or something else?
A: Nothing like that. She's just ready.

B will no doubt be puzzled. The challenge for the minimalist is to get clear on what this minimal what is said could be. We next sketch four kinds of minimalism: Weak-Minimalism, Nihilistic-Minimalism, Mysterious-Minimalism, and Relativistic-Minimalism.

3.4.3 Option 1: Weak-Minimalism

According to Weak-Minimalism, the minimal what is said expressed by an utterance of 'Alice is ready' is true as long as Alice is ready for *something*. The minimal what is said expressed by 'Naomi is smart' is true as long as Naomi is smart by *some standards* (or relative to some comparison class). We call this version of minimalism 'weak' because according to it, the minimal what is said is very easily made true. All it takes is that Alice is ready to take her next breath of air (or blink her eyes) or that Naomi is smart by some very low standard.[1]

---

[1] Conversely, 'Alice is not ready' is almost impossible to make true since Alice is always ready for something.

Problem with Weak-Minimalism: Remember, the minimal what is said is introduced to be the what is said that is shared across contexts—that can be preserved in memory and be easily reported on. It was supposed to account for the evidence of shared content in Chapter 2. The problem for Weak-Minimalism is that the minimal what is said, as she construes it, isn't something anyone would want to *assert*: it would be pointless information. Take as an example the minimal what is said that is expressed by 'Alice is ready' according to the weak-minimalist, i.e. *that Alice is ready for something*. This isn't information anyone would care about: it's trivial. What matters is the contextually enriched what is said, e.g. *that Alice is ready to go to school* or *that Alice is ready to do her homework*. That enriched information is, after all, what the speaker aims to convey to her audience.

3.4.4 Option 2: Nihilistic-Minimalism

Some minimalists (e.g. Sperber and Wilson 1995, Carston 2002, Bach 2006, Soames 2005) have offered a second option: they *deny* that the minimal what is said can be true or false. On this view, the minimal what is said expressed by an utterance of 'Alice is ready' isn't yet something that describes a way the world can be. It doesn't tell you something about the world. The minimal what is said is a kind of *frame*, or *skeleton*, on which you can build a what is said that can be true or false; that is to say, build a what is said that describes the world. What context does is add an element that completes the skeleton, and makes it into a full-blown what is said.

In the two illustrations above involving 'smart' and 'ready', the nihilistic minimalist is like the weak-minimalist until it comes to describing what is required for the truth or falsity of the minimal what is said. The nihilistic minimalist denies that the minimal what is said for 'Naomi is smart' is that *Naomi is smart by some standard* and that the minimal what is said for 'Alice is ready' is that *Alice is ready for something*. Instead, Sperber and Wilson, Bach and Soames say that the minimal what is said cannot be true or false. It is said, but it isn't the kind of thing that can correctly or incorrectly describe the world—it cannot be true or false.

Problem with Nihilistic-Minimalism: It should be clear that the concern is the same as for Weak-Minimalism. Since, according to the

Nihilists, the minimal what is said doesn't tell us anything at all (they don't describe the world), it is impossible to see that they can be worth preserving in memory or passing on in testimony.

Summary of problem for weak and nihilistic minimalism: One way to summarize the problems with the first two options is this: There's a kind of lurking instability in the 'sharability' data. We want to say both:

i. It's important to us to be able to share what is said across contexts, because that's how we give and retrieve information,
ii. It's super-easy in many cases to do this sharing.

But the very easiness threatens to undermine the reasons we want to share. If we can get testimonial information that Alice is ready so easily, without having any context that sets out what Alice is ready for, we should worry that we aren't getting the kinds of things from testimony (i.e., actually usable information) that we wanted.

3.4.5 Option 3: Mysterious-Minimalism

According to the version of minimalism presented in Cappelen and Lepore (2005) the minimalist should give a very deflationary answer to the question: what does it take for the minimal *Alice is ready* to be true? The answer should simply be: *it is true just in case Alice is ready*. When pushed on what that means, the Cappelen and Lepore-style minimalist refuses to answer. She says: *I've told you all I have to say*. Similarly, the minimal what is said expressed by 'Naomi is smart' is *that Naomi is smart.* This minimal what is said is either true or false, according to Cappelen and Lepore. It is true if Naomi is smart and false it she isn't. Don't say more, is Cappelen and Lepore's advice to the minimalist.

The obvious concern here is that this isn't very helpful. It is uninformative. Suppose you wonder: What exactly do these minimal what-is-said's tell us about the world? What is it to be ready, but not for any contextually supplied activity? What is it to be smart, but not by any contextually supplied standards (or comparison class)? The answer you get from the mysterious minimalist is, for each minimal what is said, something of the form "S' is true just in case S'. That reply is unlikely to remove your puzzlement. It looks like again it is left a mystery why such contents are worth preserving in memory or passing on in testimony.

Cappelen and Lepore (2005) try to rebut this objection. Their central response goes as follows: if pressed on, for example, the question what it is to be ready, *simpliciter*, the Mysterious-Minimalist should explain why it is not her job to answer that question. It is because, in general, it is not the job of the theorist of meaning to tell us anything substantive about the conditions under which what we say is true. Consider Jill's utterance of 'Water is liquid'. Suppose a meaning theorist concludes that in uttering that sentence, Jill says *that water is liquid*. Now consider the objection: That is insufficient as an account of what was expressed. To tell us what Jill said, you also have to tell us what it is to be liquid and what it is to be water. Surely, Cappelen and Lepore say, this is an unfair demand. It is unfair to demand from the meaning theorist that she provide answers to questions about what liquids are. That's a question for the physicist and the chemist. If we demanded such answers, then the meaning theorist would need a theory of the entire universe to present her theory of meaning and communication. That is clearly an unreasonable expectation. The same point applies to sentences containing 'ready' or 'smart' or any other context-sensitive expression: we have no good reason for expecting the theories of meaning to tell us what it is to be any of these things.

One might worry that the problem facing the first two versions of minimalism returns here: why would these mysterious what is saids be worth preserving in memory and passing along in testimony? If, as Cappelen and Lepore claim, we can't give anything but trivial accounts of what they say about the world (*that Alice is ready* is true just in case Alice is ready), why should such contents play an important role in communication? Insofar as this concern is still live, it looks like mysterious-minimalism is no great advance over the two first versions of minimalism.

3.4.6 Option 4: Relativistic-Minimalism

The word 'relativism' has been used in very many ways throughout the history of philosophy. Over the last 10–15 years or so, a new use has emerged—a use where what is called 'relativism' is a version of what we have called minimalism. For some of these newfangled relativists, the goal is to resolve the tension between the data in Chapters 1 and 2. The innovative component of relativism comes in response to the questions:

how do we assess minimal contents as true or false? How can such minimal contents be true or false? In response the relativist says: *we assess minimal propositions as true or false relative to contextually varying standards— these standards are not part of what is said, but they come in when we assess for truth or falsity.* So one and the same minimal proposition can be true relative to one context and false relative to another. This contrasts with the three earlier options outlined above: there was no suggestion that the minimal propositions differed in truth value across contexts.

Here is a slightly more elaborated outline of the view:

Relativism in a nutshell: Consider the sentence 'Building a snowman is fun'. On the one hand, 'fun' is one of those words that seem sensitive to context: what counts as fun will depend on, for example, the speaker's sense of what is fun. So, following the line of thought from Chapter 1, one might think that different utterances of 'Building a snowman is fun' will say different things in different contexts—what is said depends on what the speaker thinks is fun (the speaker's standard of fun, if you will). On the other hand, it also looks like people who speak in different contexts, with different standards of 'fun', can share information and disagree. If Jill tells you *that building a snowman is fun* and Naomi tells you *that building a snowman is not fun*, they have given you *conflicting information*. There is some common content that Jill affirms and Naomi denies. They disagree. Moreover, you can assess them, i.e. you can ask yourself: who is right, Jill or Naomi?

How can we have both sensitivity to the speaker's standards and have shared content across speakers (a content they can disagree over)? The relativist's response is this:

The differing standards will not affect the minimal what is said. There is one thing that Jill affirms and Naomi denies, i.e. *that building a snowman is fun.* This is why relativism is a version of minimalism: the relativist postulates a minimal what is said by an utterance of 'Building a snowman is fun' that is cross-contextually stable (unaffected by the standards of fun that vary between contexts). The contextually varying standards for fun only come into play when we assess what was said for truth or falsity. Suppose you, our reader, hear Jill utter 'Building a snowman is fun'. When you try to determine whether what she said is true or false, you do so using your standard of what is fun. If you don't think that building a snowman is fun, you will judge what Jill said as false and you will be right. But if Jill thinks it is fun, then she will judge it as true, using her standard. You are both right. The minimal proposition is false relative to your standard/context and true relative to her standard/context. It is important to note that you are both right. But you disagree (because one of you thinks snowman building is fun and the other does not). So the variability data from Chapter 1 is taken to show not that different things are said, but that standards of truth vary between contexts.

3.4.7 Problems for Relativistic-Minimalism

The literature on the many versions of relativism is now vast and we will not here make an effort to survey all the many objections to that view (for some critical views see the further reading section at the end of this chapter). We will briefly sketch two objections that are easy to grasp knowing just what we have outlined above.

(i) Relativism Fails to Account for the Stability Data: Does this version of minimalism do better with respect to the central objection to the previous three versions? A central point pushed throughout Chapter 2 was that we need a way to keep track of information across contexts and transmit that information in new contexts. If what we say is massively context-sensitive, then it is hard to see how we can do that. Does relativism really help resolve that problem at all? Consider this utterance by Jill:

- Samantha had fun

Suppose Nora heard Jill say this. On the picture we get from the relativist, it is easy for Nora to store what Jill said in memory—she just needs to remember the sentence. What it says is stable across contexts. It is also easy for her to tell others what Jill said: all she needs to do is utter that sentence again and then she has said what Jill said. However, something important is missing: the point of Jill's utterance was to say something contextually determined about the kind of fun Samantha had (e.g., the kind of fun four-year-olds have on a playground, not the kind of fun a philosopher has at a conference). That aspect of what Jill said is not preserved in the stable what is said we get from the relativist. So yet again, there's a concern that minimalism fails to deliver what Chapter 2 was looking for.

(ii) The 'Too Radical' Objection: According to the relativist, Jill can say that building a snowman is fun and Alex can say that building a snowman is not fun and both of them can be right. This is not because Jill says that it is fun for Jill and Alex says that it isn't fun for Alex. According to the relativist, Alex denies exactly what Jill affirms. So one and the same saying is true at Jill and false at Alex. This is a view many will retreat to only if there are no other options. But there are other options. We have presented the relativist as motivated by the tension between the stability and variability data and if that's the motivation, all the options sketched earlier in this chapter could do the same work.

CENTRAL POINTS IN CHAPTER 3

- There is a puzzle about how the data in Chapter 1 can be reconciled with the data in Chapter 2.
- Three strategies for solving the puzzle: Appeal to similarity, appeal to parasites, and appeal to minimalistic pluralism.
- Minimalistic pluralism can be spelled out in various ways, depending on how one construes the minimal what is said. Four options are considered: Weak, mysterious, nihilistic, and relativistic-minimalism.

QUESTIONS FOR CHAPTER 3

Comprehension Questions

3.1. Polly is very pedantic; she says to me 'I will arrive in precisely 9 minutes 42 seconds'. Is my report 'Polly said that she'll be here in 10 minutes' true? If so, does that support the similarity view?

3.2. Construct a case in which, by the lights of the friend of similarity, A says the same as B and B says the same as C, but such that it's clearly false that C said the same as A.

3.3. Can you think of a parasitical case involving an expression in the basic set? What about: 'John said he'd have the report on my desk 'tomorrow' but that was last Thursday.' Does that count? If not, why not?

3.4. Say in your own words what the difference between contextualism and relativism is.

3.5. Consider two utterances of 'Rotting flesh is delicious', one by a (talking) vulture, the other by a person sitting in a restaurant. Do they disagree? What does the relativist predict?

Next consider the following case from Cappelen and Hawthorne:

'Suppose a caterer says of a certain party 'That party is not going to be fun. I have to cook *hors d'oeuvres* all night'. Suppose that meanwhile, someone in a separate conversation says of the same party 'That party is going to be fun. I get to meet lots of school buddies that I haven't seen in a long time'.'

Do they disagree? What does the relativist predict?

Exploratory Questions

3.6. We have presented the radical contextualist as someone who says that 'A said the same as B' means 'A said something similar to B'. Could she, instead, say that 'A said the same as B' is false if what they say is not identical? If so, it would turn out that many of our speech reports are false: does that matter?

3.7. How does parasitism work? Can it be overridden? See examples of override in Cappelen and Hawthorne (2009).

3.8. Much of the text above focused on saying-reports (people saying what others have said). We want you now to compare such saying-reports as agreement and disagreement reports.

Consider two utterances, by A and B, of 'Nicola went to a nearby beach' uttered at two different locations (and so context anchors 'nearby' to different locations). We have observed in the main text that it seems fine to collectively report A and B with: 'A and B said that Nicola went to a nearby beach'. Homophonic reports are easy. Compare this to how we do collective agreement and disagreement reports: 'A and B agree that Nicola went to a nearby beach'. Is that fine? If not, why not?

Consider similarly a case where A and B face each other and A says (thinking of his left): 'The ball went off the left end of the table' and B says (thinking of his left): 'The ball did not go off the left end of the table'. If C were to report this by saying, 'A and B disagree about whether the ball went off the left end of the table', would that be correct? If not, why not?

Finally, consider the following cases from Cappelen and Hawthorne (2009, p. 55):

Case One: A sincerely utters, 'Nicola is smart since she stands way back against strong servers' as a comment solely on her tennis skills. B sincerely utters, 'Nicola is not smart. She invested all her money in penny stocks' as a comment solely on her business acumen.

Is the report 'A and B disagree about whether Nicola is smart' correct?

Case Two: A sincerely utters, 'Nicola is ready since she has her coat on and so we can leave now' and B says, 'Nicola is not ready since she hasn't studied enough to take the exam tomorrow'.

Is the report 'A and B disagree about whether Nicola is ready' correct?

7. Why does parasitism not work for 'I' or 'here' or other basic cases?

> FURTHER READING FOR CHAPTER 3

For more on the similarity response, see Heck (2002) and Recanati (2004).

For more on parasites, see Cappelen and Hawthorne (2009), Chierchia and McConnell-Ginet (2000, chapter 7), and Heim and Kratzer (1998, chapter 9).

For an alternative perspective on minimalism, see Borg (2006).

For more on the primary argument for pluralism, see Cappelen and Lepore (2005), Wettstein (1981), and Lewis (1980).

For some alternatives, see von Fintel and Gilles (2008) and Braun and Sider (2007).

For discussion of the import of the data, see Reimer (1998) and Richard (2008).

For some work on relativism, see Richard (2004), MacFarlane (2005), Egan, Hawthorne, and Weatherson (2005), Lasersohn (2005), and Koelbel (2002). Further work includes MacFarlane (2014) and Cappelen and Hawthorne (2009).

For a more introductory text, see Cappelen and Huvenes (forthcoming) and Cappelen and Dever (forthcoming).

PART II
Theories of Context Sensitivity

In the first part of this book, we have focused primarily on a puzzle about *communication*. We began with some observations about the meanings and truth values of sentences, but from there moved on to discuss what people *say with* and *understand by* uses of those sentences. Centrally, we have asked how we can make sense of *our ability* to talk to each other across contexts, if our language is massively context sensitive. Of course, questions of how people communicate with language cannot be kept wholly separate from questions about what the language they are communicating with means. For example, the Radical Contextualist thinks that we can't really pass information from one context to another. That's a claim about people and what they can and cannot communicate. But in discussing how the Radical Contextualist might invoke contextual parasitism in defending her view, we end up discussing talking about the interpretation of particular words. We say, for example, that in "John said Alex is ready", the speech-reporting context created by "John said" causes contextual parasitism, and results in "ready" getting its meaning from *John's* context, rather than from *ours*.

In the second part of the book, we turn to looking in more detail at what words and sentences mean. The goal is to give a *theory of meaning* for the language—a theory that can then help us understand how the meanings of our words serve our communicative goals. Our main goal here is to set out and compare two major approaches to a theory of meaning for context-sensitive language: the *character-and-content* approach due to

David Kaplan and a family of *indexed truth* approaches found in the work of David Lewis and others. The shift to thinking more about the functioning of language and less about the use of that language by speakers means that we will need to think in more detail about the *internal functioning* of the language: how the meanings of whole sentences are determined by the meanings of their component parts and the interactions among those meanings. We begin this section with a chapter discussing what we want a theory of meaning to do, and what such a theory might look like. In the next two chapters, we develop in detail meaning theories in the character-and-content and indexed truth traditions. Along the way we track how these theories differ *formally* and how they differ in the way they answer philosophical demands on a theory of meaning. The central goals of this part of the book are achieved by the end of Chapter 6, but in Chapters 7 and 8 we go on to consider how indexed truth accounts can be made more conceptually and technically sophisticated to deal with objections coming from the Kaplan tradition, and extract lessons about the relation between philosophical motivations and formal theorizing.

4

What is a Theory of Meaning?

4.1 Where We Are and the Plan for This Chapter

In Chapter 1, we saw many different kinds of context-sensitive behavior in language. In this section, we turn to the question of how a theorist might build a *theory of meaning* for a language that deals with context sensitivity. But we can't even get started on building a theory of meaning for context sensitivity until we figure out what kind of thing a theory of meaning is. In this chapter, we introduce some tools for building a very simple theory of meaning. With those tools in place, in the next few chapters we consider how things need to be changed and complicated to fit context sensitivity into the theory.

Before we can say what a theory of meaning *is*, we need to say what a theory of meaning is *supposed to do*. So we begin this chapter by considering what our goals are in giving such a theory. There are many ways of trying to meet those goals. Here we focus on one particular style of meaning theory, one that approaches meanings centrally through the notion of *truth*. We thus introduce the ideas of *truth conditions* and *possible worlds* as tools for explaining truth conditions. We then discuss the idea that a good theory of meaning should be *compositional*, showing how the meanings of whole sentences are determined by the meanings of their component words. The truth-conditional framework we set out then allows us to make a distinction between *rigid* and *nonrigid* terms. This distinction, although it might appear a mere technical curiosity at first, is of considerable philosophical importance, and plays an important role in our discussion of context sensitivity in subsequent chapters. Finally, we make a few brief remarks about the place of a truth-conditional theory of meaning in the larger enterprise of theorizing about language and communication by introducing the distinction between *semantics* and *pragmatics*.

4.2 What Are We Trying to Do with a Theory Of Meaning?

We want a theory of meaning so that we can systematize, explain, and predict something. But what? There is a lot that we could ask of a theory of meaning. A *total theory of language* would give us tools for explaining and understanding full communicative exchanges of the form:

> Speaker has some communicative goals. She has some beliefs she wants to convey to Hearer, some emotional states she wants to induce in Hearer, some topics that she wants to make prominent in the conversation, some signals about relative social status between her and Hearer she wants to send. She assembles some sentences that are suitable for those communicative goals, combining what she knows about what combinations of words are grammatical, what individual words mean, how those word meanings interact with each other in grammatical combination, what Hearer expects her to say, how various candidate sentences carry various cultural evocations, and so on. When she says her selected sentences, Hearer then reacts to those sentences in various ways. He finds various sentences polite or impolite, ambiguous or unambiguous, true or false, surprising or unsurprising, relevant or irrelevant. He extracts from the sentences bits of information together with suggestions, presuppositions, and evocations. In response to all of this, he adopts some new beliefs about the world, changes his expectations about Speaker's future actions, alters his plans, and shifts his mood.

Giving a total theory that can account for all of this is an enormous task, one that likely spans across linguistics, philosophy, psychology, sociology, and neurology. We aren't going to do anything like that. Instead, we will select a few key features of such a total theory that are of particular importance in understanding context sensitivity, and build a toy theory showing how we might start theorizing about these features.

4.3 What is Said and Truth Conditions

Our starting point is the two inter-related notions of what is said and *truth conditions*. When Alex utters the sentence 'Snow is white', there is something that she says—namely, *that snow is white*. She says that snow is white, in particular, by using a sentence that *means* that snow is white. The connection between what is said by a *speaker* and what is said by a *sentence* is a controversial matter, especially in light of the issues of pluralism discussed in the previous chapter. But to have a starting point for theory building, we will begin with the assumption that what is said by a sentence has a certain kind of priority—that what a speaker says in uttering a sentence is determined by what that sentence says. This is certainly a simplification (and in the discussion of semantics and pragmatics below we will gesture toward some ways of reducing the simplification), but it will prove a useful simplification.

We have talked repeatedly about what is said by a sentence or a speaker. But what are these things, the what is saids? There is no uncontroversial answer to this question. Some theorists take what is said to be a complex of objects and properties. Others take what is said to be a type of mental act or event, or a special sort of fact or state of affairs, or an abstract object of some sort. We won't try to adjudicate this difficult issue here. Rather, we will focus only on some theoretical roles for what is said by a sentence. Here are two important ones:

A. What is said by sentences helps to characterize sentences as *saying the same thing* or *saying different things*, and to characterize speakers as *agreeing* or *disagreeing*. For example, we might think that the sentences 'Alex loves Beth' and 'Beth is loved by Alex' say the same thing, while 'Alex loves Beth' and 'Beth loves Alex' say different things. We thus want what is said by a sentence to track this data, so that two sentences say the same thing if and only if what is said by the first sentence is identical to what is said by the second sentence. We can then use what is said to explain patterns of agreement and disagreement. If Charles says 'Alex loves Beth' while Danielle says 'Beth is loved by Alex', then Charles and Danielle agree with each other, because what is said by Charles' sentence is the same thing as what is said by Danielle's sentence. But if Charles says 'Alex loves Beth' and Elizabeth says 'Beth loves Alex', then Charles and Elizabeth do not agree, because what is said by their two sentences differs.

B. What is said by a sentence helps explain its truth *value* and truth *conditions*. The sentence 'Snow is white' is true, and the sentence 'Grass is orange' is false. The truth values of these sentences are a result of two things: what the sentences says, and the way the world is. If the word 'snow' picked out carrots, rather than a form of frozen precipitation (a change in meaning), then 'Snow is white' would not be true. If grass contained high levels of carotenoids, rather than high levels of chlorophyll (a change in the world), then 'Grass is orange' would be true. So a theory of meaning should do some of the work of predicting and explaining truth values of sentences.

Because truth values are determined by a combination of what the sentence says and the way the world is, what is said by a sentence lets us go from the way the world is to the truth value of the sentence. The sentence 'grass is orange' says *that grass is orange*. Grass isn't orange, so the sentence isn't true. But grass could have been orange, so the sentence could have been true. What is said by a sentence tells us how the world must be for the sentence to be true. The *truth conditions* of a sentence tell us the truth value of that sentence in each state of the world. The actual truth value of the sentence is then a result of combining its truth conditions with the actual state of the world to see if the actual state meets those conditions.

What a sentence says thus determines when that sentence says the same thing as other sentences, and the truth conditions of that sentence. A good theory of meaning, then, will tell us for each sentence what is said by that sentence, and what the truth conditions for the sentence are. Because we are remaining neutral about what kind of thing is *said* by sentences, we will focus more on truth conditions. In telling us what a sentence says, a theory also tells us its truth conditions. If we know that the sentence 'Schnee ist weiss' says that snow is white, then we thereby know its truth conditions: it is true whenever snow is white. But it will be helpful to have another way to talk about truth conditions.

4.4 Possible Worlds

Consider two things we want to do with truth conditions:

> A. Some sentences *imply* other sentences. From 'Alex is both happy and hungry', we can infer 'Alex is happy'. These implication relations are important to know about, because they enable us to reason with the information we get through language. And these implication relations are a consequence of the meanings of sentences. It is because of what 'Alex is both happy and hungry' means and what 'Alex is happy' means

that the first sentence implies the second. Implication relations are an important part of the data we use in constructing a good theory of meaning for a language.

Implication relations should be determined by truth conditions. But we need to say more about truth conditions for them to do explanatory work here. Suppose, for example, we want to explain the fact that 'Alex is both happy and hungry' implies 'Alex is happy'. The truth conditions of the first sentence are that Alex is both happy and hungry, and the truth conditions of the second sentence are that Alex is happy. That in itself won't get us far in seeing that the first implies the second. If we're uncertain whether Alex could be both happy and hungry without Alex being hungry, then we'll be uncertain whether the first truth conditions can be met without the second also being met.

B. We want to be able to calculate the truth conditions of complex sentences based on the truth conditions of their component parts. Knowing the truth conditions for 'Alex is happy' should be helpful in determining the truth conditions for 'Alex is *not* happy'. But we can't give a systematic account of such calculations without first having a richer picture of what truth conditions are. We can say already, of course, that the truth conditions of 'Alex is happy' are that Alex is happy, and that the truth conditions of 'Alex is not happy' are that Alex is not happy. But saying that doesn't say anything that gets us started calculating from one truth condition to the other.

Here is another way of thinking about truth conditions. The sentence 'Alex is happy' is true—Alex has had a pleasant day, the weather is beautiful, and she is generally cheerful. But the sentence could have been false. Had Alex received a rejection letter from the graduate school she applied to, the sentence would have been false. There are many ways things could have been. The way things actually are, salt dissolves in water. But things could have been otherwise. There is another way things could have been, in which the ionic attraction in salt is stronger, or the dipole nature of water molecules is weaker, in which salt doesn't dissolve in water.

Some ways things could have been are *maximal* ways things could have been. One way things could have been: it's raining in Edinburgh. But this isn't a maximal way things could have been, because we can expand it to a larger (more fully descriptive) way things could have been. Things could have been such that it's raining in Edinburgh, and sunny in Aberdeen. This still isn't maximal, because it can be expanded to a way such that it's raining in Edinburgh, sunny in Aberdeen, and snowing in Moscow. And so on. But eventually we'll reach a description of a way things could have been that is so rich that if we try to add anything more to it, it will no longer be possible that things could have been that way. (We'll end up saying, for example, both that it's raining in Edinburgh and that it's sunny in Edinburgh.)

Let's call maximal ways things could have been *possible worlds*. Then we can talk about a sentence being true or false *in a possible world*. We will say that a sentence S is true in a possible world W just in case, had things been the W way, S would have been true. One maximal way the world could be is the full way that it actually is. Call this way the *actual world*. The sentence 'snow is white' is true in the actual world. But there are also ways things could have been, such that snow reflected predominantly light in the 700-angstrom range. Let W1 be a world that is that way. In W1, snow is red, rather than white. So 'snow is white' is false in W1.

Each sentence then has a profile of truth values in different possible worlds. We call this profile the *intension* of the sentence. We can think of intensions in either of two interchangeable ways:

1. The intension of a sentence can be thought of as a *rule* determining its truth value at each world. Intensions thought of in this way associate 'graphs' with sentences:

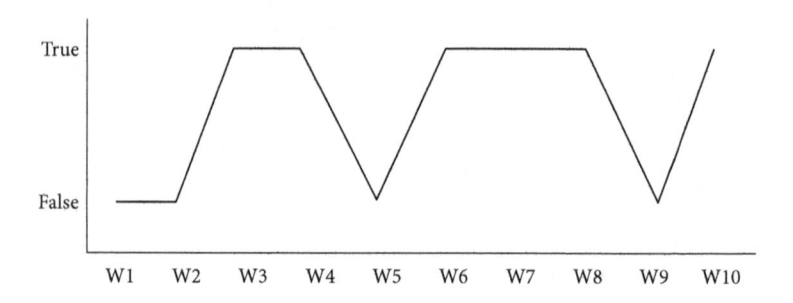

2. The intension of a sentence can be thought of as a set of worlds: all the worlds at which the sentence is true. Intensions thought of in this way can be represented as 'regions of logical space':

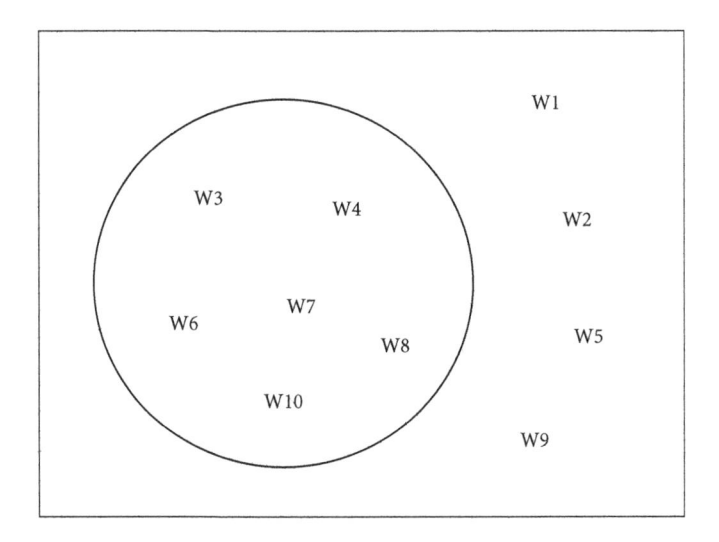

```
┌─────────────────────────────────────────┐
│                                         │
│              _____                   │
│            /          \       W1        │
│           /            \                │
│          |  W3    W4    |      W2       │
│          |              |               │
│          |    W7        |               │
│          | W6     W8    |      W5       │
│           \            /                │
│            \  W10    /                  │
│             _____/       W9           │
│                                         │
└─────────────────────────────────────────┘
```

For our purposes, we will use intensions as formally precise versions of truth conditions. The *extension* of a sentence is then the truth value that its intension determines in the actual world.

4.5 Compositionality

If we think of truth conditions as intensions, then we can say some helpful things about how truth conditions for complex sentences are calculated from the truth conditions of their parts. Suppose we have an intension for the sentence 'Alex is happy' and an intension for the sentence 'Beth is sad'. Thinking of these intensions as sets of worlds, we can give a simple diagram representing both intensions:

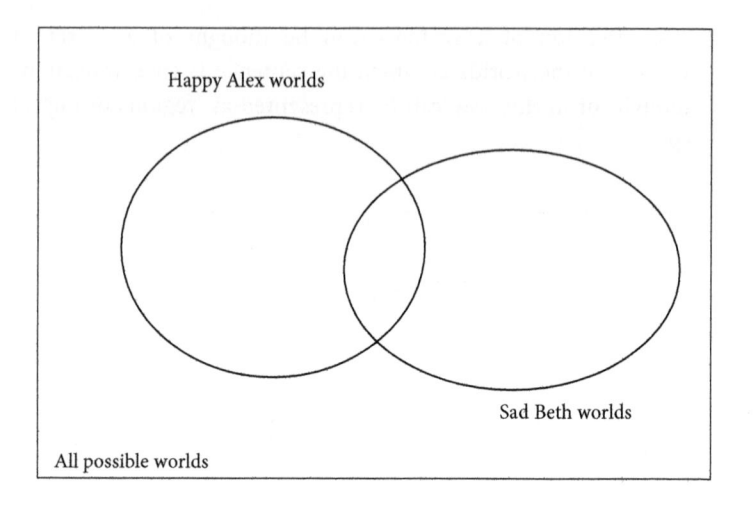

[Diagram: A rectangle labeled "All possible worlds" containing two overlapping ellipses labeled "Happy Alex worlds" and "Sad Beth worlds".]

Given this diagram, what is the intension of the complex sentence 'Alex is happy and Beth is sad'? Clearly it should be the *overlap* of the two intensions:

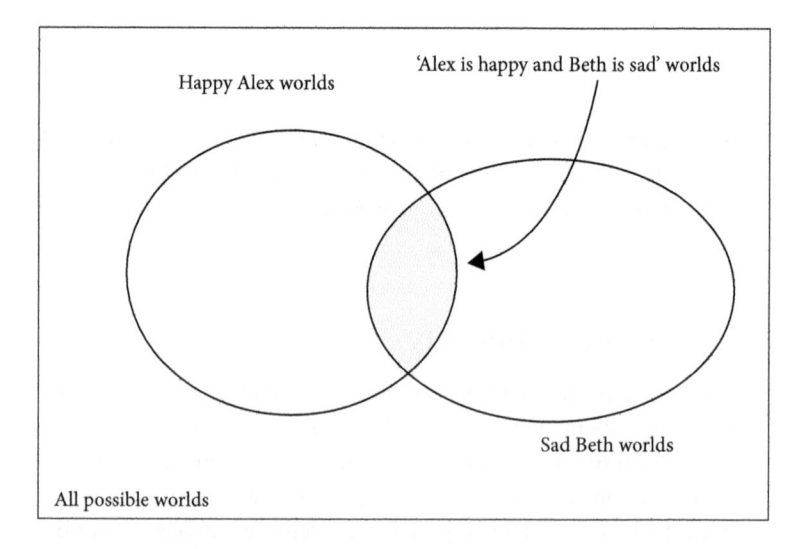

[Diagram: A rectangle labeled "All possible worlds" containing two overlapping ellipses labeled "Happy Alex worlds" and "Sad Beth worlds", with the overlapping region shaded and labeled "'Alex is happy and Beth is sad' worlds".]

Giving the truth conditions of 'Alex is happy' and 'Beth is sad' as sets of worlds thus allows a systematic calculation of the truth conditions of more complex sentences built up from those simple sentences.

This sort of calculation is a particular instance of a general *principle of compositionality*.

> **Compositionality**: A theory of meaning is compositional if the meanings of complex expressions (like 'Alex is happy and Beth is sad') are fixed by the meanings of the parts of those complex expressions (like 'Alex is happy' and 'Beth is sad'), along with the way in which those parts are put together.

Because we are asking our theory of meaning to tell us the intensions of expressions, compositionality then requires that the intensions of complex expressions be fixed by the intensions of their parts. Compositionality helps explain our ability to understand an infinite number of sentences in a language. This infinite capacity of ours derives from our knowledge of the meanings of each of finitely many words, together with our knowledge of compositional rules for combining those meanings to form meanings of full sentences.

If we were setting out more than a toy theory here, we would need to develop detailed procedures for calculating meanings of sentences from the meanings of the parts of those sentences. We care more about the *concept* of a compositional theory of meaning than about all of the details of building such a theory, so we'll give only a few brief examples. The discussion of 'Alex is happy and Beth is sad' suggests a general rule for combining sentences with 'and':

> (**And Rule**): Suppose we have two sentences S and T, and we know the intension of S and the intension of T. Then there is another complex sentence 'S and T', formed by joining S with T using 'and'. The intension of 'S and T' is then fixed by the intension of S and the intension of T:
> - 'S and T' is true in a given world if and only if S is true in that world and T is true in that world.
> - Equivalently, the intension of 'S and T' is the *intersection* of the intension of S and the intension of T: it is the overlap of those two intensions, all the worlds that are in both intensions.

The (And Rule) is a general rule because we can apply it to any two sentences we want, substituting them for S and T. If we take S to be 'Alex is happy' and T to be 'Beth is sad', then the (And Rule) produces the result we obtained above for 'Alex is happy and Beth is sad'. If we take two other sentences, the (And Rule) will tell us that the intension of their conjunction is the intersection of their intensions.

The (And Rule) is only one small part of a full theory of meaning, of course. To apply the (And Rule) to two sentences, we need already to know the intension of those sentences. The (And Rule) tells us that the intension of 'Alex is happy and Beth is sad' is the intersection of the intension of 'Alex is happy' and the intension of 'Beth is sad', but the (And Rule) won't tell us what the intension of 'Alex is happy' is—other parts of the theory of meaning will need to do that.

Once we see how to give a rule like the (And Rule), we can give similar rules for other expressions. For example, we can give a rule for the word 'not':

(**Not Rule**): Suppose we have a sentence S whose intension we know. Then there is a complex sentence 'Not-S', formed by combining the word 'not' with S. The intension of 'Not-S' is then fixed by the intension of S:
- 'Not-S' is true in a given world if and only if S isn't true in that world.
- Equivalently, the intension of 'Not-S' is the *complement* of the intension of S: it is the exterior of the circle of S worlds, all the worlds that are not in the intension of S.

The (And Rule) and (Not Rule) allow us to calculate intensions of whole sentences from intensions of other (simpler) whole sentences. But we also need to explain how truth conditions of the simplest sentences are derived from the meanings of their parts. For example, the sentence 'Alex is happy' is true in a given world just in case the person that the word 'Alex' picks out in that world is one of the people that 'is happy' picks out in that world. Just as sentences have truth values in worlds, terms have referents in worlds, and predicates are satisfied by various objects in worlds. Every expression, then, has its own intension—its own rule determining what its extension (its normal meaning) is in each world. Our theory of meaning will also have:

(**Alex Rule**): In every world, 'Alex' refers to Alex.

(**Happy Rule**): In every world, 'happy' picks out the set of people that are happy in that world.

4.6 Truth and Consequences

Once we have truth conditions, we can put them to work for us. Consider the sentence 'Alex is happy and Alex is not happy'. Suppose we have an intension for 'Alex is happy' (represented by the shaded circle):

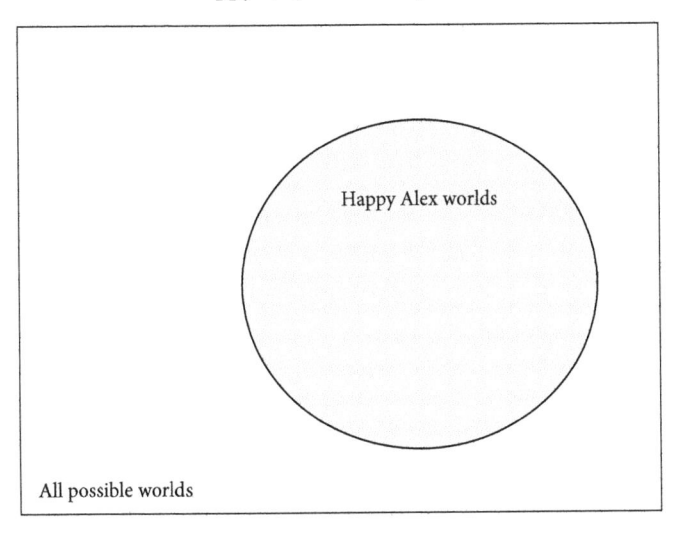

[Diagram: a box labeled "All possible worlds" containing a circle labeled "Happy Alex worlds".]

Then we can find the intension of 'Alex is not happy' by taking the complement of the intension of 'Alex is happy'. This gives us everything outside the circle:

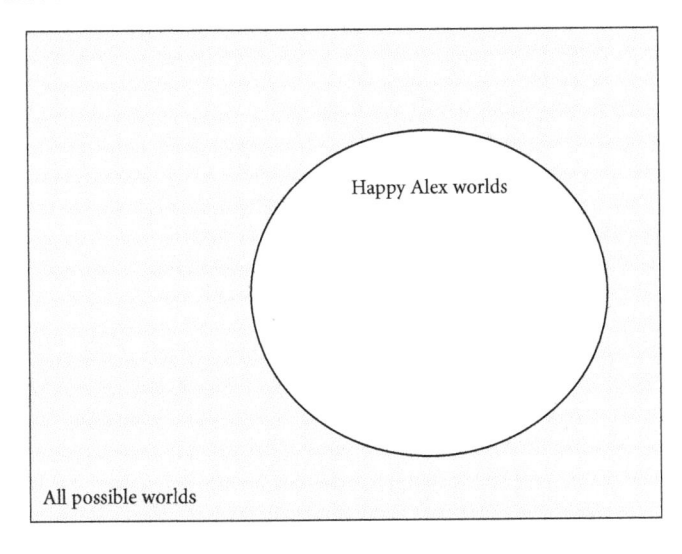

[Diagram: a box labeled "All possible worlds" containing a circle labeled "Happy Alex worlds".]

The intension of the conjunction 'Alex is happy and Alex is not happy' is then the intersection of those two intensions. But there is no overlap between the interior of the circle and the exterior of the circle, so the intension of 'Alex is happy and Alex is not happy' is empty. The conjunction is not true in *any* world. This shows that the sentence is a contradiction. Of course, we knew that already, but now the tools of our simple theory of meaning allow us to predict and explain its contradictory status.

We can also capture logical implication with our theory. A premise implies a conclusion just in case the truth of the premise guarantees the truth of the conclusion. So we can say:

Implication: A sentence P implies a sentence C if and only if every world in which P is true is also a world in which C is true.

Consider the following diagram:

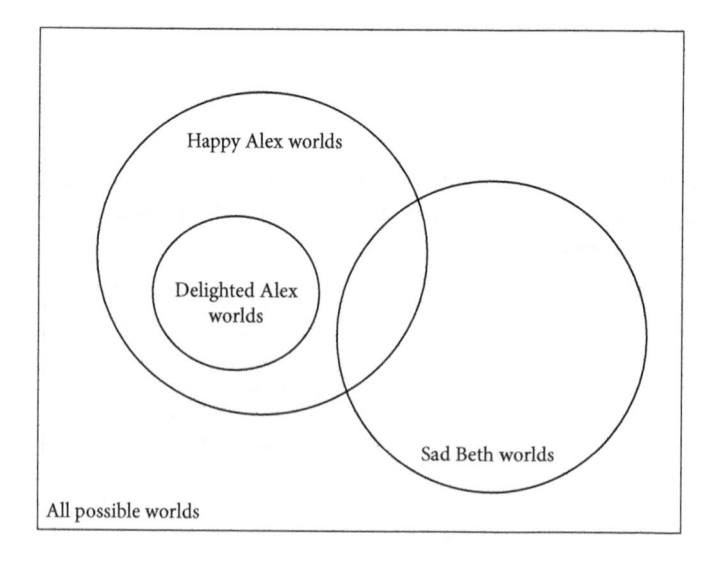

[Diagram: A rectangle labeled "All possible worlds" contains a large circle labeled "Happy Alex worlds" with a smaller circle inside labeled "Delighted Alex worlds". Another circle labeled "Sad Beth worlds" overlaps with the "Happy Alex worlds" circle.]

According to this diagram, 'Alex is delighted' implies 'Alex is happy', because every world in which 'Alex is delighted' is true is a world in which 'Alex is happy' is true. But 'Beth is sad' does not imply 'Alex is happy', because there are worlds in which 'Beth is sad' is true but 'Alex is happy' is not true. For P to imply S, then, is for the intension of P to be a *subset* of the intension of C—for the P worlds to be entirely contained in the C worlds. (Our diagram represents another rather implausible implication relation—see if you can find it.)

We've now seen the broad outline of a possible worlds truth-conditional theory of meaning. By combining the (Alex Rule), the (Happy Rule), the (And Rule), and the (Not Rule), we can calculate in a compositional way the truth conditions of sentences built up from the words 'Alex', 'happy', 'and', and 'not', and use those truth conditions to discover and explain inferential relations between those sentences.

4.7 Rigidity

Introducing intensions allows us to make an important distinction between *rigid* and *nonrigid* terms. Suppose Alex is the tallest person in the room. Then the following two sentences have the same truth value:

(Alex) Alex is a philosopher.
(Tall) The tallest person in the room is a philosopher.

But although Alex *is* the tallest person in the room, she might not have been. Shaquille O'Neal might have been in the room as well. In a world in which Shaq is also in the room, 'the tallest person in the room' picks out him, not Alex. As a result, in that world 'The tallest person in the room is a philosopher' is not true. (We assume that despite Shaq's nickname, 'The Big Aristotle' is not, in fact, a philosopher.) But in this world, it is still true that *Alex* is a philosopher. Putting Shaq in the room as well doesn't change Alex's academic background.

So the sentences (Alex) and (Tall) have the same extension, but different intensions. In the Shaq world, (Alex) is true and (Tall) is false, so they do not have the same truth value in every world. The two sentences differ in intension because the two terms 'Alex' and 'the tallest person in the room' differ in intension. Like (Alex) and (Tall), 'Alex' and 'the tallest person in the room' have the same extension, since they both in our world pick out the same individual (namely, Alex). But in the Shaq world, 'the tallest person in the room' no longer picks out Alex. Instead, it picks out Shaq. That's why (Tall) is false in that world. Alex's continuing status as a philosopher becomes irrelevant to the truth value of (Tall) in the Shaq world, and instead it's Shaq's non-philosopher status that matters.

The term 'the tallest person in the room' has a *non-constant* intension. Who 'the tallest person in the room' picks out changes from world to world. That's because 'the tallest person in the room' picks out a person in a world *descriptively*. It picks out whoever in a given world has a certain feature. Since the features of objects can change from world to world (in one world, Alex has the feature *being tallest in the room*, in another world she does not), who gets picked out by this expression can change. In general, terms of the form 'the so-and-so' will have non-constant intensions.

In the Shaq world, the referent of 'the tallest person in the room' changes, but the referent of 'Alex' doesn't change. 'Alex' continues to pick out Alex, even when she is not the tallest person in the room. In fact, 'Alex' picks out Alex in *every* world. That's because the word 'Alex' doesn't pick out someone in virtue of *how* she is, but rather in virtue of *who* she is. And in every world, Alex is Alex. The intension of the word 'Alex' is thus *constant*. It is a function that picks out the same object in every world.

Terms with constant intensions are called *rigid*. One symptom of rigidity is the way terms interact with expressions like 'might', 'must', and 'could' which cause sentences to be evaluated in other worlds. Compare the following two sentences:

(Tall*) The tallest person in the room could have been the shortest person in the room.

(Alex*) Alex might not have been Alex.

(Tall*) is true. Whoever is *in fact* the tallest person in the room could have lacked that feature. In some worlds they are shorter, and in others they are in rooms with other taller occupants. But (Alex*) is false. No matter how Alex changes from world to world, she is always Alex. So 'Alex' is rigid, and 'the tallest person in the room' is not.

(Don't fall into a tempting confusion. You might think: but Alex isn't Alex in *every* possible world, because in some possible worlds she is named 'Beth', or 'Shaquille O'Neal', or 'John Jacob Jingleheimer Schmidt'. It's true that Alex's name could have been different. And in a world in which Alex is named 'Beth', people don't talk about Alex when they say 'Alex is a philosopher'. But we are not concerned with the language spoken by residents of the 'Beth' world, but rather with our own language, and in our language, the word 'Alex' continues to pick out Alex, even in the 'Beth' world. That's why we can describe the 'Beth' world as a world in which *Alex* is named 'Beth'—we can still use our word 'Alex' to pick out Alex in that world, and then say how people in that world refer to her. See Question 10 at the end of the chapter for more on this issue.)

As a general rule, proper names like 'Alex' are rigid, while descriptive phrases like 'the tallest person in the room' are nonrigid. It is useful for languages to have both rigid and nonrigid expressions, because we track the things in the world we want to talk about in two different ways. Sometimes there is a specific object in the world we want to talk about (such as Alex), but we don't know all of the many features of that object, especially in other possible worlds. So we want a linguistic tool for picking out that object that isn't sensitive to those features. For these purposes, we use a rigid expression. At other times there is a *role* that we care about (such as *being the tallest person in the room*), but we don't know who occupies the role, especially in other possible worlds. So we want a linguistic tool for picking out the object playing that role that *is* sensitive to those features. For these purposes, we use a nonrigid expression.

Following Kripke's classic discussion in *Naming and Necessity*, rigidity has come to be seen as a linguistic property with important ramifications in a number of areas in metaphysics, epistemology, and philosophy of language. As we will see, questions about rigidity drive important theoretical decisions about how to extend the preliminary picture of the theory of meaning we are giving in this chapter to a theory that also includes context sensitivity.

4.8 Semantics and Pragmatics

A good theory of meaning will tell us what is said by each sentence in the language, and will compositionally assign truth conditions for every sentence. But it is common to think that the full task of saying what is communicated by a sentence is more than we should try to do in a theory of meaning. To use a famous example, consider the professor who writes a letter of recommendation for a student that says 'Jones is very punctual to class, and has excellent handwriting'. In some important sense that letter *communicates* that the professor does not think highly of Jones (else more, and more relevant, information would have been given in the letter). But there is a clear task for a *theory of meaning* that goes no further than saying that the meaning of 'Jones is very punctual to class and has excellent handwriting' is that Jones is very punctual and has excellent handwriting.

It is thus common to distinguish between the *semantic theory* that tells us what a sentence means from the *pragmatic theory* that tells us what people convey by using the sentence. How to distinguish between semantics and pragmatics is a notoriously difficult matter, on which we take no stance here. We just focus on what the semantic theory needs to look like, for whatever portion of the data ends up getting classified as semantic. In the next chapter, we will turn to the question of how to adapt the ideas of this chapter for the purpose of giving a semantic theory for context-sensitive language. But before building a theory for the *semantics* of context sensitivity, there is a question about how much context-sensitive behavior should get a specifically semantic explanation. Consider a few examples which contrast semantic and pragmatic styles of explanation:

1. As we saw in Chapter 1, a very large class of expressions seems to be context sensitive. To take an example not discussed before: In some contexts (ones in which we are concerned with Frank's obesity), to say 'Frank weighs 200 pounds' is to say something that depends only on Frank's organic body, not on his clothing and metallic implants. In other contexts (ones in which we are concerned with whether the elevator is overloaded), to say 'Frank weighs 200 pounds' is to say something that depends on his body, clothing, and implants. To treat this context-sensitive behavior as part of the *semantics* is to say that the literal truth conditions of the sentence change from one context to another—there is no stable level of content. This in turn may require saying that the name 'Frank' in one context picks out just the body, but in another context picks out body and accoutrements. Or it might require saying that the word 'weigh' picks out different relations in the different contexts. To treat this context-sensitive behavior as part of the *pragmatics*, on the other hand, is to say that there is a constant context-insensitive semantic meaning of the sentence—what we in Chapter 3 called the minimal content—and that we exploit that constant meaning for our communicative purposes differently in different contexts. Perhaps the semantic (i.e. minimal) meaning of the sentence is that Frank's organic body weighs 200 pounds, but we count on our audience's ability, in the elevator context, to see that the clothing is relevant and that we are speaking loosely.

2. In some contexts (ones in which we are talking to our undergraduate class), to say 'Everyone is getting a good grade' is to say that everyone *in the class* is getting a good grade. In other contexts (ones in which we are at a university-wide meeting about grade inflation), to say 'Everyone is getting a good grade' is to say that everyone *in the university* is getting a good grade. To treat this context-sensitive behavior as part of the *semantics* is to say that the literal truth conditions of the sentence change from one context to another. This in turn might require saying that the quantifier 'everyone' changes its range of quantification from one context to another, or saying that there is a hidden context-sensitive expression that means 'in the class' in one context, and 'in the university' in the other context. To treat this context-sensitive behavior as part of the *pragmatics*, on the other hand, is to say that there is a constant context-insensitive semantic meaning of the sentence, and that we exploit that constant meaning for our communicative purposes differently in different contexts. Perhaps the semantic meaning of the sentence is that *absolutely everyone* is getting a good grade, but we count on our audience's ability in context to see that we can't plausibly seriously intend a claim that absolutely everyone is getting a good grade, and to assume that we are for convenience and simplicity failing to specify a restricted group of people, and to find a plausible candidate for that restricted group.
3. In some contexts (ones in which Alex is speaking), the sentence 'I am happy' says something about Alex. In other contexts (ones in which Beth is speaking), the sentence 'I am happy' says something about Beth. To treat this context-sensitive behavior as part of the *semantics* is to say that the literal truth conditions of the sentence change from one context to another, and hence to say that the referent of the word 'I' changes from one context to another. To treat this context-sensitive behavior as part of the *pragmatics*, on the other hand, is to say that there is a constant context-insensitive semantic meaning of 'I am happy'. It's very hard to see what a reasonable candidate for that meaning could be—perhaps it is a sort of 'incomplete meaning' that doesn't have a specified subject. (See the discussion of nihilistic minimal content in Chapter 3.) That incomplete meaning is then exploited by the speaker on the assumption that the audience can figure out, in context, a plausible

completion of it. Because of the difficulty in giving a plausible constant picture of what is said by 'I am happy', this sort of context sensitivity is almost universally thought to be part of the semantics.

We won't try to settle these semantics/pragmatics questions here. From here on out, we will address only questions about the semantics of context sensitivity. For any particular example we give, of course, there is the possibility of arguing that it should be treated as part of the pragmatics. But as long as we think that there is *any* part of context sensitivity that needs a semantic analysis, our particular examples can always be replaced with suitable ones lying within the semantic part of the project.

> CENTRAL POINTS IN CHAPTER 4

- A theory of meaning tells us what is said by sentences and under what conditions sentences are true or false.
- *Truth conditions* can be understood as rules saying whether sentences are true or false relative to possible worlds, where possible worlds are maximal ways things could have been.
- Truth conditions are a special case of a more general theoretical category of *intensions*. Intensions are rules saying what expressions of any sort pick out relative to possible worlds.
- A theory of meaning should be *compositional*. It should show how the meanings, such as intensions, of complex expressions can be calculated from the meanings of the parts of those expressions.
- We can distinguish between the project of *semantics* (to say what sentences mean) and the project of *pragmatics* (to say what speakers convey by using those sentences). Context sensitivity exists in both semantics and pragmatics.

> QUESTIONS FOR CHAPTER 4

Comprehension Questions

4.1. We drew a distinction between what a sentence says and what a speaker says in uttering it. Can you think of a case in which these come apart?
4.2. Which of the following pairs of sentences stand in the implication relation?

(a) In my office, I dropped the pen; the pen fell at 32 feet per second
(b) 2+2=4; 99−9=90
(c) It's false that I didn't sign the document; I signed the document
(d) George Eliot wrote *Middlemarch*; Mary Ann Evans wrote *Middlemarch*
(e) Josh is Herman; Dundee is beautiful
Are these all good results?

4.3. Consider the sentences 'Every tall philosopher owns a red car' and 'Every philosopher owns a red car'. Does either sentence imply the other? What about 'Some tall philosopher owns a red car' and 'Some philosopher owns a red car'?

4.4. Give compositional rules similar to the (And Rule) and the (Not Rule) for 'S or T' and for 'If S, then T'. Then using the rules for "and", "or", and "not", show that 'S or not S' is true in every possible world, and show that 'S and T' and 'not (not S or not T)' are true in exactly the same possible worlds.

Consider how satisfactory the compositional rule for 'If S, then T' is. Give an example of an English conditional sentence whose meaning is not well analyzed by that rule.

4.5. As noted above, definite descriptions, terms of the form 'the so-and-so', generally have non-constant intensions. Give some examples of definite descriptions with constant intensions.

4.6. We claim above that names have constant intensions. Are there exceptions to this? Consider the name 'Jack the Ripper', introduced as a name for whomever committed the Whitechapel murders in 1888. Is the name 'Jack the Ripper' rigid or nonrigid?

4.7. Is there an analog of rigidity for verbs or sentences? Is it interesting or important if so?

Exploratory Questions

4.8. Build a chart of data by checking implication relations between sentences of the forms:
(a) [Every/some/no/most/few/the/any/three] tall philosopher(s) own(s) a red car.
(b) [Every/some/no/most/few/the/any/three] philosopher(s) own(s) a red car.
Then do the same for sentences of the forms:
(c) [Every/some/no/most/few/the/any/three] tall philosopher(s) own(s) a red car.
(d) [Every/some/no/most/few/the/any/three] tall philosopher(s) own(s) a car.
What might we learn about the meanings of quantifier words like 'every', 'some', and 'no' from this data?

4.9. We have remained neutral here on what kinds of things what is saids are. But one possibility is that what is said by a sentence just is the intension of that

sentence. That would mean that any two sentences with the same intension say the same thing. Discuss why the following pairs of examples cause problems for identifying what is said with intensions:
(a) Superman can fly.
(b) Clark Kent can fly.
and:
(c) 1+1=2.
(d) 7 is prime.
Would it help if we had worlds in which Superman was not identical to Clark Kent? What are the considerations for and against allowing such worlds?

4.10. Consider a possible world in which people speak a language called 5-lish. 5-lish is much like English, but in 5-lish the word 'four' is used to pick out the number 5 (that is, the number of fingers on a normal hand), and the word 'five' is used to pick out the number 4 (that is, the number of legs on a normal cat). When people in this world say 'Two and two make five', they speak truly, and express the truth that we would express by saying 'Two and two make four'. So there is a sense in which 'Two and two make five' is true with respect to the 5-lish world. But there is another sense in which it is false. The 5-lish world differs from the actual world in the meanings of some words, but it doesn't differ in the properties of mathematics, so what we express when we say 'Two and two make five' is false in the 5-lish world. Let's distinguish between a sentence being true at a world if the sentence would be true if uttered by the speakers of that world, and being true in a world if the sentence (as uttered by us) describes how things would have been if the world had been actual. For each of the following examples, determine whether the given sentence is true at and in the given world:
(a) Quentin was so-named by his parents because he was their fifth child. In the world Sixth-Child, his parents had more children, and he was their sixth child. Consider the truth value of 'Quentin is happy' both in and at Sixth-Child.
(b) Christmas is Susan's favorite day of the year. In the world Early-Christmas, Christmas is celebrated on December 24, rather than on December 25. Consider the truth value of 'Today is my favorite day of the year', uttered on December 25, both in and at Early-Christmas.
(c) Albert points at the Eiffel Tower and says 'That is the tallest building in France'. In the world Arc-Point, Albert is instead pointing at the Arc de Triomphe. In the world Short-Tower, Albert is pointing at the Eiffel Tower, but the Tour Montparnasse is taller than it is in the actual world, and in particular is taller than the Eiffel Tower. Consider the truth value of 'That is the tallest building in France' both in and at both Arc-Point and Short-Tower.

4.11. Quantifier domain restrictions can vary from context to context, as in the example above of 'Everyone is getting a good grade'. But quantifier domain restrictions can also vary due to another quantifier in the sentence, as in 'In each of my classes, everyone is getting a good grade'. Some philosophers take this kind of variation as evidence that the context sensitivity of quantifier domain restriction is semantic, rather than pragmatic. Examine the quality of this evidence. In doing so, you might consider two questions:
   (a) Whether other types of context sensitivity display the same ability to be influenced by quantifiers in the sentence, and where those types seem to be on the semantic-to-pragmatic spectrum.
   (b) Whether other types of clearly pragmatic phenomena can interact with quantifiers and other logical operators in a sentence.

FURTHER READING FOR CHAPTER 4

For further reading on the nature of what is said, King (2011), King, Soames, and Speaks (2014).

For a standard textbook on the theory of meaning, see Heim and Kratzer (1998).

For theories of meaning without possible worlds, see Davidson (1967) and its textbook presentation in Larson and Segal (1995).

For alternatives to theories of meaning based on truth conditions see Greenberg and Harman (2008), Horwich (1998), Heim (1982), and Kamp (1981), each of which depart more or less dramatically from the theory developed here.

For rigidity, see the classic Kripke (1980), LaPorte (2006).

For more on compositionality, see Pagin and Westerstahl (2010).

For pragmatics, see the essays in Grice (1989), Korta and Perry (2015), Bach (2004).

5

Character and Content

5.1 Where We Are and the Plan for This Chapter

In the previous chapter we sketched a simple picture of a theory of meaning: it tells us what each sentence says, and thereby also assigns to each sentence truth conditions, in the form of an intension giving the truth value of that sentence in each possible world. In this chapter we set out the most common way of adapting such a theory of meaning to deal with context sensitivity, as developed by David Kaplan (1977/1989) in his paper "Demonstratives".

The sentence 'I am a philosopher' is context sensitive, because it is true when spoken by Elizabeth Anscombe but false when spoken by George Bush. But what does its context sensitivity tell us about its *meaning*? 'I am a philosopher' cannot be straightforwardly treated with the tools of the previous chapter. Is 'I am a philosopher' true or false in the actual world? It depends on who is saying it. To say this is to say that we can't give the sentence (all by itself, not as spoken by anyone in particular) a truth value in the actual world. So if our original picture of meanings was as something responsible for determining intensions, we're going to need to change, and complicate, our picture.

Kaplan's theory uses two levels of meaning: *character* and *content*. In this chapter, we set out Kaplan's distinction between character and content, and show how that distinction allows incorporation of context-sensitive language into a truth-conditional theory of meaning. We then discuss a number of theoretical benefits that come with a Kaplanian theory, showing that it accounts well for the role of context sensitivity in communication and action. Kaplan's theory produces a novel empirical prediction: that no language will contain a distinctive sort of expression that Kaplan calls a *monster*. We close this chapter by explaining Kaplan's notion of a monster and considering whether Kaplan is correct in predicting that human languages are monster-free.

5.2 Kaplanian Theory of Meaning

Kaplan's picture of the mechanics of context sensitivity begins with a simple idea. The problem is that we can't give a once-and-for-all intension or truth value to a context-sensitive sentence like 'I am a philosopher'. The reason for this is that the sentence says *different* things in *different* contexts, and so has different intensions in different contexts, and different truth values in different contexts. So we need to supplement our basic account of meaning. Rather than assigning a single what is said to a context-sensitive sentence, we need to assign a *rule* that determines, in each context, what that sentence says in that context.

The result is a *two-stage* theory of meaning:

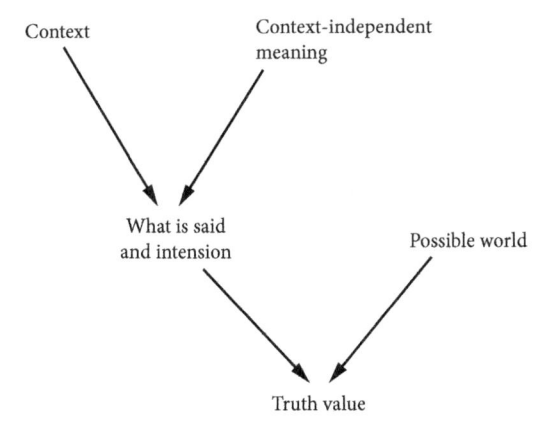

```
Context          Context-independent
                 meaning
     \              /
      \            /
       v          v
      What is said
      and intension            Possible world
            \                  /
             \                /
              v              v
              Truth value
```

We start with a context-independent meaning for each sentence. This meaning is a rule that tells us, for any given context, what is said by that sentence as used in that context. Given what is said by the sentence in that context, we also have truth conditions and an intension. The intension is another rule: this time a rule that tells us, for any given possible world, whether the sentence is true or false in that world.

In Kaplan's two-stage theory, the positions in the above diagram labeled 'context-independent meaning' and 'what is said and intension' are called *character* and *content*. So:

i. The *character* of a sentence determines the *content* of that sentence in each context.
ii. The *content* of a sentence in a given context determines the truth value of that sentence, as used in that context, in each world.

As Kaplan originally presents his picture, contents are taken to be intensions, and hence themselves rules for determining truth values of sentences (in contexts) in worlds. But an obvious modification of Kaplan's approach takes contents to be what is said, which then determine intensions, and characters to be rules giving what is said in context. On this picture, what you learn when you learn what a sentence means is its character. Knowing its character then enables you to determine the content expressed by that sentence in any given context.

Let's work through an example. Consider the sentence 'I am now happy'. Consider two contexts:

- In the Alex-27 context, the sentence is uttered by Alex on May 27.
- In the Beth-28 context, the sentence is uttered by Beth on May 28.

The character of the sentence 'I am now happy' determines a content for each of these utterances. As used in Alex-27, the content is *that Alex is happy on May 27*, which then yields the intension that determines the sentence to be true in any world in which Alex is happy on May 27. So if Alex is happy in the actual world on May 27, but unhappy in some alternative possibility on May 27, then 'I am happy', as uttered in Alex-27, says something true in the actual world and false in the alternative possibility. As used in Beth-28, the content is *that Beth is happy on May 28*, which then yields the intension that determines the sentence to be true in any world in which Beth is happy on May 28. When the one sentence 'I am now happy' is used in two different contexts like this, we have only *one* character, but *two* different contents. In this case, despite saying the same sentence, Alex and Beth do not agree with one another.

But suppose Beth says 'You are now happy' in a context of Beth-27-Alex—a context of May 27 with Beth as speaker and Alex as audience. Then Beth's sentence produces the content *that Alex is happy on May 27*. Her sentence has a different character from the sentence 'I am now happy'. Had Beth said 'I am now happy' in Beth-27-Alex, she would have produced the content *that Beth is happy on May 27*. But her utterance of 'You are now happy' in Beth-27-Alex agrees with Alex's utterance of 'I am now happy' in Alex-27. These two examples show us that:

- Same character, different content → No agreement
- Different character, same content → Agreement

It is then natural to extend the two-stage character-and-content view to all sentences of the language, whether context sensitive or not. The character of 'I am a philosopher' is a *non-constant* rule, that determines one content (*that George Bush is a philosopher*) in one context and a different content (*that Elizabeth Anscombe is a philosopher*) in another context. The character of 'Kripke is a philosopher', on the other hand, is a *constant* rule that determines the same content (*that Kripke is a philosopher*) in every context. There is an analogy with the distinction between rigid and nonrigid expressions:

Rigid expressions: same extension in every possible world	Constant character expressions: same content in every context
Nonrigid expressions: different extensions in different possible worlds	Non-constant character expressions: different content in different contexts

We can also talk about character and content for individual words. For simplicity, we can take the content of an individual word (in a context) to be an intension. The character of the word is then a rule determining its content in each context. Just as non-context-sensitive sentences have constant characters yielding the same content for every context, non-context-sensitive *words* have constant characters yielding the same content for every context. The word 'I' has a non-constant character, while the word 'Aristotle' has a constant character.

5.3 Philosophical Payoffs of the Character–Content Distinction

The Kaplanian framework gives us two kinds of meaning: characters and contents. One immediate advantage of a two-stage theory is that it gives us tools to capture the sameness-and-difference nature of context sensitivity. When there are multiple utterances of 'I am a philosopher' in different contexts, there is something the same about all of these utterances. They all have the same character. It is because they all have the same character that it is possible to learn a context-sensitive language without traveling around to every possible context. But there is also something different about the utterances. They all have different contents, by virtue of having their common character determine, in combination with different contexts, different referents for 'I' and hence different truth conditions. But there are a number of less obvious benefits to the two-stage structure. We discuss four of those benefits here.

1. **Agreement and Disagreement**. Any adequate theory needs to be able to explain the following facts:
    A. Two people can fail to agree even when they both utter the same sentence.
    B. Two people can fail to disagree even when they utter sentences that are negations of one another.
    C. Two people can agree even when they utter different sentences.
    D. Two people can disagree even when they do not utter sentences that are negations of one another.

    Characters are not helpful for capturing these facts about agreement and disagreement. When Bush and Anscombe each utter 'I am a philosopher', they make use of the same character, but they do not thereby agree. But contents do capture agreement and disagreement facts. The content of Bush's utterance is *that Bush is a philosopher*, and the content of Anscombe's utterance is *that Anscombe is a philosopher*. The contents are different, so we correctly predict that there is no agreement. On the other hand, when Alex says 'I am happy', and Beth says to Alex 'You are happy', their utterances both have the content *that Alex is happy*, and we correctly predict that there is agreement.

2. **Kaplanian Logical Truths**. Characters let us capture some distinctive features of sentences that contents miss. Consider the sentence 'I am here now'. There is clearly something distinctive about that sentence—it has a certain kind of *inevitability* to it. But if 'I am here now' is uttered by Alex on May 27 in St Andrews, then the character of the sentence, combined with the context of utterance,

produces the content *that Alex is in St Andrews on May 27*. And there's nothing distinctive or inevitable about that content. In particular, that content is contingent. There are worlds in which Alex *is* in St Andrews on May 27, and there are worlds in which Alex *is not* in St Andrews on May 27.

The distinctiveness of 'I am here now', then, is not that an utterance of that sentence expresses a metaphysical necessity (something that is true in every possible world). But any utterance of that sentence is true, and there is an *epistemological* distinctiveness to it. If you think to yourself, 'I wonder if I am here now', you should quickly realize that you don't have to do any investigating of the world to figure out that, indeed, you are. This distinctiveness is not brought out at the level of content, but it is at the level of character. In any context of utterance C, 'I' picks out the speaker in C, 'here' picks out the location of C, and 'now' picks out the time of C. So the character guarantees that the content determined, *when evaluated in the actual world*, will be true. (In Chapter 8 we discuss *answering machine cases* which show that Kaplan may need an additional distinction between *proper* and *improper* contexts to capture the special status of 'I am here now'.)

3. **Cognitive Significance**. When Alex thinks 'I am in danger', and Beth thinks regarding Alex 'You are in danger', they think thoughts with the same content—namely, *that Alex is in danger*. By virtue of that sameness of content, they in one important sense *think alike*. But in another important sense, they do not think alike. Alex has a thought that motivates her to action in a particular fashion—perhaps it causes her to duck under the table. Beth doesn't react to her thought that Alex is in danger by ducking under the table, though. Rather, her thought (despite having the same content as Alex's thought) motivates her to call the police.

On the other hand, when Alex thinks 'I am in danger' and Beth thinks 'I am in danger', they think thoughts with different content. Alex's thought has the content *that Alex is in danger*, while Beth's thought has the content *that Beth is in danger*. But despite that difference of content, they in another important sense *think alike*. Alex's thought and Beth's thought both motivate them to action in the same way—they are both motivated to duck under the table.

The *cognitive significance* of a thought is the characterization of the way that it motivates the thinker to action. What these two examples show, then, is that two thoughts with the same content can have different cognitive significance, and two thoughts with different content can have the same cognitive significance.

An adequate account of cognitive significance is an important component of an overall account of belief and its place in the theory of the mind. One important point of assigning meanings to mental states is to use those meanings in predicting and explaining patterns of behavior, and if the meanings we assign don't capture cognitive significance, then they won't contribute to that important goal. But because content doesn't track with cognitive significance, we can't use truth-conditional meaning to serve this goal. The two-stage structure of Kaplanian theories, however, gives us another useful tool. Perhaps *character* determines cognitive significance. When Alex and Beth both think 'I am in danger', they think thoughts with the same cognitive significance, and also with the same character. When Alex thinks 'I am in danger' and Beth thinks of Alex 'You are not in danger', they think thoughts with different cognitive significances and also with different characters. If character can play the role of cognitive significance, that is an important victory for the Kaplanian framework and its ability to integrate the linguistic theory of meaning with the mental theory of meaning.

Observation #5.1

The correlation between cognitive significance and character in the case of much context-sensitive language is intriguing and suggestive, but there remain substantial obstacles to having a full theory. Two brief worries:

A. Coreferential proper names can differ in cognitive significance. Lex Luthor's thought 'Superman is approaching' may motivate him to action in a way different from his thought 'Clark Kent is approaching'. But 'Superman' and 'Clark Kent' have the same content (namely, rigid reference to the mild-mannered reporter/superhero) in every context, and hence have the same character. In general, it is hard to see how character can track cognitive significance for non-context-sensitive expressions, given that such expressions always have constant characters.

(continued)

Observation #5.1 *Continued*

B. Alex's thought 'Alex is in danger' has different cognitive significance from her thought 'I am in danger', as can be seen by the possibility that the first thought would not motivate Alex to action, when she has lost track of who she is. That means that it can be true that Alex believes 'Alex is in danger', but false that Alex believes 'I am in danger'. Given that "Alex is in danger" and "I am in danger" (in a context with Alex as speaker) have the same content, it must be the difference in character that makes the difference in the truth values of the belief reports. But a difference in the truth values of the belief reports means a difference in the *content* of the belief reports. That means that belief reports must allow some sort of integration of characters into the process of determining contents. Substantial technical challenges face any attempt to spell out the details of such integration.

4. **Rigidity.** Does Kaplan's theory simply amount to saying that 'I' means 'the speaker of the context'? No—there is an important difference between 'I' and the 'the speaker'. To take an example of Kaplan's, suppose Alex thinks to herself, 'I wish I were not speaking'. If 'I' simply meant 'the speaker', then Alex's thought 'I wish I were not speaking' would be the unsatisfiable wish 'I wish the speaker were not speaking'. But Alex's wish can be satisfied.

The difference between 'I' and 'the speaker' is that 'I' is *rigid*, while 'the speaker' is not. Once the context has settled who the referent of 'I' is, then 'I', like a proper name such as 'Aristotle', picks out that same individual in every possible world. The rigidity of 'I' explains why Alex can think of herself in other possible worlds using 'I' without needing to worry about whether she, in those other possibilities, continues to meet some description.

Because 'I' is rigid, it refers to the same person (given a context) with respect to every possible world. So 'I could have been Plato', as spoken by Aristotle, is not made true by the possibility that Plato is speaking. On the other hand, 'I' also resembles a nonrigid phrase like 'the tallest man' in having a *descriptive nature*. In the case of 'I', the descriptive nature is something like 'the speaker of the context', or 'the producer of the utterance'. So there is a puzzle about how to fit together the rigid behavior of context-sensitive expressions with the fact that for such expressions, there is a descriptive rule determining how context settles their meaning.

The separation of character and content lets us accommodate both rigidity and descriptive nature. We need to be able to give a rule saying how a word like 'I' gets its meaning from context. That rule needs in some way to specify that 'I' refers to the speaker in the context. But we don't want that rule to get into the *content*, because the content might get evaluated with respect to a world in which the rule picks out someone different (because someone else is speaking, or because no one is speaking at all). By having a separate level of character, we provide a place to put the rule so that it won't interact with changing possible worlds in the wrong way.

Observation #5.2

We have just been emphasizing that context-sensitive expressions like 'I' are rigid, and showing how Kaplan's distinction between character and content allows an explanation of that rigidity. But not all context-sensitive expressions are rigid. Consider the pair of expressions 'tomorrow' and 'the next day'. Both of these are context sensitive, and at first they might appear to be equivalent. The sentences:

1. Tomorrow is Wednesday.
2. The next day is Wednesday.

are both true when used in a Tuesday-context, and false when used in a Thursday-context. However, when we combine 'tomorrow' and 'the next day' with further time specifications like 'on Monday', we discover a difference between them:

3. John told me on Monday that he would turn in his paper tomorrow.
4. John told me on Monday that he would turn in his paper the next day.

If both of these sentences are uttered on Thursday, the first says that John committed to turning in the paper on Friday (and is still on time), while the

(continued)

Observation #5.2 *Continued*

second says that John committed to turning in the paper on Tuesday (and is already late). The difference emerges here because:

- 'Tomorrow' is rigid. Once context provides a day for it to refer to, it always refers to that day, even if expressions like 'on Monday' change the time under discussion in the rest of the sentence.
- 'The next day' is not rigid. It gets an initial value from context, but then when expressions like 'on Monday' change the time under discussion in the sentence, 'the next day' changes to follow suit.

We see the same contrast with the pair 'I' and 'the speaker', and with 'you' and 'the audience'.

Once we see that there are nonrigid as well as rigid context-sensitive expressions, we see that the Kaplanian framework needs a method for accounting for the *lack* of rigidity of (e.g.) 'the next day' as well as for the rigidity of (e.g.) 'tomorrow'. One method for creating nonrigid behavior:

A nonrigid context-sensitive expression like 'the next day' in context picks out not a specific day, but rather a property of a day: the property *being the day after the time under discussion in the sentence*. At different times, or in different worlds, different days could have that property, so the behavior of 'the next day' would be nonrigid.

So the difference in rigidity between 'tomorrow' and 'the next day' is explained by the fact that in the transition from character to content, given a particular context, 'tomorrow' provides the particular day after the time of the context, and thus allows no further variation in reference, while 'the next day' just provides a descriptive tool for picking out a time relative to the time under discussion in the sentence, allowing the time referred to to change as the time under discussion changes.

Consideration of these sorts of cases shows that we need to keep separate the two distinctions (a) between constant character and non-constant character expressions, and (b) between rigid and nonrigid expressions. Consider the following table:

(continued)

> **Observation #5.2** *Continued*

	Rigid	Nonrigid
Constant Character	'Aristotle'. In any context, the character of 'Aristotle' yields an intension that picks out Aristotle in every world.	'The tallest man'. In any context, the character of 'the tallest man' yields an intension that picks out, in each world, whatever man is tallest in that world.
Non-constant Character	'I'. In a given context, the character of 'I' yields an intension that picks out, in every world, the speaker of that context.	'The book I am reading'. In a given context, the character of 'the book I am reading' yields an intension that picks out, in each world, whatever book is being read in that world by the speaker of the context.

5.4 Monsters and Rigidity

Kaplan's claim that 'I' is rigid is the claim that, in a given context of utterance, 'I' always picks out the same object (the speaker of that context), no matter how the word 'I' is embedded in the sentence. When 'I' is used in combination with a *modal* expression such as 'it might have been', it still picks out the speaker of the context, not someone who *might* have been speaking. When 'I' occurs within the scope of a *temporal* expression such as 'two years ago', it still picks out the speaker of the context, not someone who *two years ago* was speaking. And so on. But is it really true that 'I' is rigid in this way? Or could there be expressions that do cause 'I' to change its referent?

Kaplan (1977/1989: 510) considers the possibility of *context-shifting operators*, which he calls *monsters*:

> My liberality with respect to operators on content... does not extend to operators which attempt to operate on character. Are there such operators as 'In some

contexts it is true that', which when prefixed to a sentence yields a truth if and only if in some context the contained *sentence* (not the content expressed by it) expresses a content that is true in the circumstances of that context? Let us try it: (9) In some contexts it is true that I am not tired now.

For (9) to be true in the present context it suffices that some agent of some context not be tired at the time of that context. (9), so interpreted, has nothing to do with me or the present moment.

We have already seen in the first chapter that the context sensitivity of expressions can be brought out by *context-shifting arguments*, which consider how changes in context lead to changes in what is said. Context-shifting *operators* would then be bits of language that caused context-sensitive language to be evaluated in different contexts without actually moving to a new context. But, says Kaplan, the attempt to add context-shifting operators fails. 'In some contexts it is true that I am not tired now' does not have the context-shifting reading Kaplan is attempting—rather, it is just a somewhat odd way of saying of the speaker and his time of utterance that he is not tired at that time. Kaplan (1977/1989: 510) concludes that natural languages do not and cannot have monsters.

The absence of monsters from natural languages is on Kaplan's view a convergence of a matter of empirical observation and a matter of principle. We start with the empirical observation that there are no monsters. From this observation, we venture a general hypothesis about the meaning structure of natural languages: we conclude that natural languages implement their dual sensitivity to aspects of context in a tiered system of character and content, in which all shifting is confined to the content level. Once we endorse this general hypothesis about the broad structure of our languages, we then conclude that our languages are not monster-friendly—to add a monster to a language would require a massive restructuring of the basic architecture of the language. So we can then reasonably expect that as we continue to investigate the context sensitivity of natural languages, we will continue not to find any monstrous expressions.

Kaplan's brief example of an attempt to introduce a monster does indeed seem to fail spectacularly. 'In some contexts, I am not tired now' still talks about the actual speaker and actual time of utterance, so the 'in some context' prefix fails monstrously to switch us to a different context.

But of course one example of something that isn't a monster doesn't amount to a proof that there are no monsters. Recent cross-linguistic work has resulted in a number of suggestions of apparently monstrous constructions. Some examples:

1. In the Ethiopian language Amharic, when Jill utters the sentence we would translate as 'Naomi said that I am a hero', Jill can be interpreted either as saying that Naomi thinks that *Jill* is a hero, or as saying that Naomi thinks that *Naomi* is a hero. This second reading is the monstrous reading, the one that Kaplan predicts should not be possible. Jill is the speaker, so the context of utterance sets Jill as the value of the contextual parameter from which the word 'I' gets its referent. So 'I' should always, in that context, pick out Jill. When it instead picks out Naomi, we then have evidence that context shifting has occurred.

   Schlenker (2003) suggests that in Amharic, psychological attitude verbs such as 'thinks' are monsters, and can shift the context (not just the circumstances of evaluation) for sentences within their scope. The context is shifted to one in which the reported agent (Naomi) is the speaker of the context. Similar examples have been given in a number of other languages, including Aghem (a Bantu language spoken in Cameroon), Ewe (a Niger-Congo language spoken in Ghana and Togo), Korean, Matses (a Panoan language spoken in Peru and Brazil), Navajo (an Athabaskan language spoken in the southwestern United States), Nez Perce (a Sahaptian language spoken in the northwestern United States), Slave (an Athabaskan language spoken in northwestern Canada), Uygher (a Turkic language spoken in western China), and Zazaki (an Indo European language spoken in Turkey). Some interesting features of these constructions:

   i. The monster is some verb that has to do with thinking or saying. There is cross-linguistic variation in which verbs have monstrous effects, but the tendency is for verbs like 'said' to be more likely to be monstrous, and for verbs like 'believes' to be less likely to be monstrous.
   ii. The 'monstrosity' is typically optional. So 'Naomi said that I am a hero' has one (monstrous) reading on which the first-person

pronoun picks out Naomi, and another (nonmonstrous) reading on which the first-person pronoun picks out the speaker Jill.

iii. There is variation both across languages and within languages in which context-sensitive expressions are monstrously shifted. In Slave, for example, 'tell' shifts both first and second-person pronouns, while 'say' shifts only first-person pronouns. In some languages context-sensitive words other than pronouns, like 'here' and 'now', get shifted.

iv. There is also variation in whether the monstrosity must be uniform. Consider the sentence 'Naomi said that I saw my daughter', as spoken by Jill. Monstrosity, when a language makes it available, will allow the first-person pronouns to refer to Naomi, rather than to Jill. In a language that requires uniformity of its monsters, when there is monstrosity at all, there is monstrosity for all the context-sensitive expressions in the sentence, so the sentence does *not* have a reading on which Naomi said that Jill saw Naomi's daughter. In a language without a uniformity requirement, we can get that reading.

2. Various forms of sign language exhibit sophisticated versions of monstrous constructions. In sign languages, one mechanism for talking about and referring to objects is to set up locuses in the space in front of the signer. The signer associates a locus with a specific person or object, and then makes subsequent reference to that object by pointing to that locus. Sign languages also typically have a mechanism of *role shift*. In role shift, the signer indicates one of the locuses that have been set up (by shifting body position or eye focus). The signer thereby 'adopts the role' of the person associated with that locus. Once they have done so, uses of the first-person pronoun refer to the adopted role, not to the signer themselves.

So the signer could set up Alex in a locus, and then sign 'Alex thinks (role shift to Alex) I am a hero', using the usual first-person pronoun sign after the role shift. What would be communicated is that Alex thinks that she herself is a hero, not that Alex thinks that the signer is a hero. Or the signer could sign 'Alex (role shift to Alex) I chased a giraffe', again using the usual first-person pronoun sign after the role shift. What would be communicated is that Alex chased a giraffe. The role shift mechanism thus appears to act as a monster, changing the context so that context-sensitive expressions

are evaluated with respect to a context in which the role occupier, rather than the signer, is the agent.
3. A technique sometimes used in fictional narrative is *free indirect discourse*. In free indirect discourse, things are presented from the perspective of a character, or the thoughts of a character are given, without an explicit labeling of the narrative as a reporting of thought. Consider the following piece of narrative by an omniscient narrator:

> After I left, James collapsed exhausted into bed. He thought with dread about his upcoming meeting with Marco. He wasn't going to meet him here—he'd move to a new apartment tomorrow. That much he knew for sure; all the rest he'd figure out in the morning.

The third sentence of this narrative continues to report James' thought, but does so without saying (for example) 'James thought that' or 'James thought "..."'.

Free indirect discourse has interesting effects on context-sensitive language. Some context-sensitive language gets interpreted from the point of view of the reported agent. In the above example, 'tomorrow' picks out the day after James' exhausted collapse, not the day after the narration. And 'here' picks out James' location, not the narrator's location. But other context-sensitive language gets interpreted from the narrator's context. James' thought is reported in free indirect discourse with third-person pronouns, not first-person—if the narrator had said, 'I wasn't going to meet him here', he would inevitably be reporting about *himself*, not about James. Free indirect discourse is thus monstrous with respect to some context-sensitive language (tomorrow, here), and not with respect to other context-sensitive language (I, you).

4. Pronouns are context-sensitive expressions. But their interpretation can be shifted away from the context of utterance by being bound by quantifiers. This is obvious and uncontroversial for third-person pronouns. 'She is a philosopher', as uttered in context C, says that some woman prominent in C is a philosopher. But 'Every woman at the conference said that she was a philosopher', uttered in the same context, does not use 'she' to talk about the woman prominent in C, but rather to talk about all of the women at the conference.

In more unusual cases, we can get similar behavior from first and second-person pronouns. Consider examples such as:

- Every time I meet a philosopher, we start arguing about free will. ('We' picks out the speaker together with varying philosophers, rather than the speaker and the audience of the context.)
- Every time I teach this course, more of you get in trouble for plagiarizing your papers. ('You' picks out the varying students in the teachings of the course, not just the audience of the context.)
- (Spoken by the Pope) I'm usually Italian. ('I' picks out the many popes, not just the current speaker.)

In these cases, the phrases 'every time' and 'usually' are acting monstrously, causing the pronouns to get interpreted in a shifted context. Kaplan himself gives a similar example in a footnote as he discusses his 'no monsters' view:

- Never put off until tomorrow what you can do today.

What to make of this data about apparent monsters is a difficult empirical and theoretical question. We return in Chapter 7 to some further discussion about monsters and how they might impact our thinking about the best theory of meaning for context-sensitive language.

Kaplan's original work on the distinction between character and content came with a number of very specific commitments about context sensitivity and the nature of contexts. Kaplan was interested in a small range of indexical expressions like 'I', 'you', 'here', 'now', 'that', and 'actual', not the full range of context-sensitive expressions in language of the sort we sketched in the first chapter. And because his attention was restricted to that small range, he had a very specific picture of contexts as a short list of features suited to the items in that range. Let a *Kaplan context* be a list of a speaker, a time, a place, and a world. Kaplan contexts give a particular theory about how to represent these very general things called 'contexts' that we keep talking about. Whether it's a good theory or not we will take up in more detail in the third part of the book. But the basic insights of the two-stage framework can be largely severed from the specific commitments of Kaplan's original work, and used for the full range of context sensitivity.

CENTRAL POINTS IN CHAPTER 5

- On Kaplan's view, sentences have two levels of meaning. The first level is the *character*. Characters are context-independent, and are rules for determining the second level of meaning in each context. The second level is *content*. Contents are context-dependent, and give truth conditions for sentences in context.
- The character–content distinction can be extended to individual words. The character of 'I' is a rule giving the content of 'I' in each context; the content of 'I' in a context is the speaker of that context.
- The character–content distinction has a number of philosophical payoffs:
  i. It explains patterns of agreement and disagreement among speakers using context-sensitive language.
  ii. It predicts and explains a novel category of logical truths.
  iii. It gives tools for accounting for patterns of cognitive significance.
  iv. It explains the rigidity of certain context-sensitive expressions.
- Empirical data about so-called *monsters* in natural language present a challenge to the Kaplan framework.

QUESTIONS FOR CHAPTER 5

Comprehension Questions

5.1. Can you think of an expression with a non-constant character and a non-constant content?

5.2. Give sentences that exemplify the agreement and disagreement facts A–D in the text.

5.3. Think up another Kaplanian logical truth in addition to 'I am here now' (consider other expressions in the Basic Set). Do we want to count 'I am the speaker' as such? If not, why not?

5.4. In addition to the difference in rigidity, can you think of another reason against saying that the content of 'I' is the intension that maps a world to the speaker in that world? (Hint: think about that last description.)

Exploratory Questions

5.5. When thinking about intensions and truth values relative to worlds, we made a distinction between a sentence being true at a world and being true in a world. How should we think about the analogous issue with characters and content at a context? Suppose the sentence "Kripke is a philosopher" is uttered in a context in which the language being spoken is a variant of English, in which the word 'philosopher' means what 'mathematician' actually means. Should the character of the English sentence 'Kripke is a philosopher' specify that in such a context, the sentence has as its content that Kripke is a philosopher, or that Kripke is a mathematician?

5.6. As we saw in the previous chapter, a good theory of meaning will tell us how the intension of a sentence is determined by the intensions of its parts. Can we say similar things about the character of a sentence and the characters of its parts? Consider, for example, the rule that the intension of a conjunction is the intersection of the intensions of its component conjuncts. Is there a similar rule that the character of a conjunction is the intersection of the characters of its component conjuncts? What would the intersection of two characters be? What should the character of the conjunction 'and' be? If there is a difference between intensions and characters in the way in which features of complex expressions are determined by features of component expressions, is there any interesting consequence for our thinking about context sensitivity?

5.7. Suppose Alex is being rapidly teleported from place to place by an evil demon. Ten times every second, Alex's location is changed. While this teleportation process is going on, Alex thinks 'I am here now'. Is what Alex thinks true? Can Alex know the truth value of the thought? You can consider versions of the case in which Alex can see the change in location, or in which Alex's eyes are closed, blocking awareness of the change in location, or in which the evil demon is teleporting Alex among a large number of qualitatively indistinguishable locations.

5.8. Consider the following objection to the claim that when Alex and Beth both think 'I am in danger', they are motivated to action in the same way.

When Alex thinks 'I am in danger', she is motivated to get Alex under the table and not to get Beth under the table. But when Beth thinks 'I am in danger', she is motivated to get Beth under the table and not to get Alex under the table. Thus they are not motivated to perform the same actions.

Addressing this objection requires considering what is meant by 'acting in the same way'. How might we characterize sameness here, and what theoretical goals are fulfilled by defining it one way rather than another? Is there a natural way to characterize sameness so that Alex and Beth act the same way when Alex thinks 'Alex is in danger' and Beth thinks 'Beth is in danger'? If so, should those two thoughts have the same cognitive significance?

5.9. Consider whether the following examples using first and second-person pronouns should be treated as monsters.
- I am parked out back. (Contrast with 'My car is parked out back.')
- We might win the Superbowl this year. (Spoken by someone who is a fan of, rather than a member of, the team.)

- I am the ham sandwich. (Said to the waiter bringing out the plates.)
- You should check before you open the door—I could have been a thief.
- I thought you were my mother. (Said to someone upon answering the phone.)

What nonmonstrous alternative explanations of these cases could we give?

> **FURTHER READING FOR CHAPTER 5**

Kaplan's original paper can be found, along with a collection of other papers pertaining to it, in Almog, Perry, and Wettstein (1989).

Braun (2015) is helpful to read alongside this chapter. The separation of character and content leads to the development of 'two-dimensional' theories of meaning: see the papers in García-Carpintero and Macia (2006); for a criticism, see Soames (2005).

For purportedly monstrous sentences with indexicals in English, see Nunberg (2004).

Recent work in linguistics on presupposition, implicature, and expressivity uses Kaplan's framework as a starting point. See, for example, Potts (2005).

For more on monsters, see Schlenker (2003) and Anand and Nevins (2004).

6

Indexed Truth Accounts
An Alternative to Kaplan

6.1 Where We Are and the Plan for This Chapter

We have now explored Kaplan's distinction between character and content, seeing what a Kaplanian theory looks like, and what some of the important philosophical payoffs of such a theory are. Kaplan's approach to the theory of meaning for context sensitivity was for many years the dominant one in philosophy. But recently alternative approaches, following on from important work by David Lewis and Robert Stalnaker, have become increasingly influential. These alternative approaches present quite different pictures about how context sensitivity interacts with theories of truth and communication, and have played important roles in the disputes between contextualist and relativist explanations of various linguistic phenomena.

In this chapter we set out the core of these alternative approaches. They question whether we need separate stages of character and content, and suggest that we can make do with a single level of meaning. We show that in its simplest form this sort of *Indexed Truth* account is subject to two problems that the Kaplanian account does not face. The Indexed Truth theory does not account for the rigidity of context-sensitive expressions, and it does not yield a satisfying account of what is said by context-sensitive sentences, and hence of patterns of agreement and disagreement among speakers. In Chapters 7 and 8, we discuss more sophisticated versions of Indexed Truth theories that fix those two problems.

The fixes to the problems are not just *repairs*, trying to even the score with the Kaplanian picture. They are the beginnings of importantly different ways of organizing a theory of meaning. The final result is a theory that thinks of successful communication in a way quite different from the way Kaplan does. The alternative model of communication has a flexibility to it that allows a better account of how informative communication occurs in cases that Kaplan's theory views as uninformative, and provides a framework that is friendly to the Pluralist pictures discussed in Chapter 3.

6.2 Kaplan, Content, and the Operator Argument

According to Kaplan's theory, context sensitivity shows us that we need a dramatic change to the way we give a theory of meaning for a language. Our starting thought was that a theory of meaning just had one job: it assigned truth conditions to sentences in the language. But Kaplan argues that a theory of meaning needs to do two things. It assigns *characters* to sentence types, and *contents* to utterances of those sentence types in contexts. When we introduced Kaplan's theory in the previous chapter, we didn't say much about what Kaplanian contents are. We made do with the pre-theoretic neutral formulation in which we picked out contents by specifying what is said by an utterance. So we said that the content of an utterance of 'I am happy' in a context in which Alex is speaking is *that Alex is happy*, since that is what is said by Alex with that sentence in that context. But we didn't worry about what *kind of thing* that content was.

Now it's time to be more precise, and say what Kaplanian contents are. We will then see that there is an instability lurking in Kaplan's preferred theory of contents, and exploring that instability will point us toward an alternative picture of the semantics of context sensitivity. One obvious possibility is that we could take our formal model of what is said from Chapter 4 and use it as Kaplanian content. The content of a sentence in a context would then be a set of possible worlds, or to put it another way, a function from possible worlds to truth values.

If we think about it in this way, then Kaplan's two-stage theory provides meanings for context-sensitive language that can be thought of as a sequence of machines. The first machine is the *character* machine. This machine lets you insert a context, and then provides you with another machine: the *content* machine. The content machine then lets you insert a possible world, and provides you with a truth value.

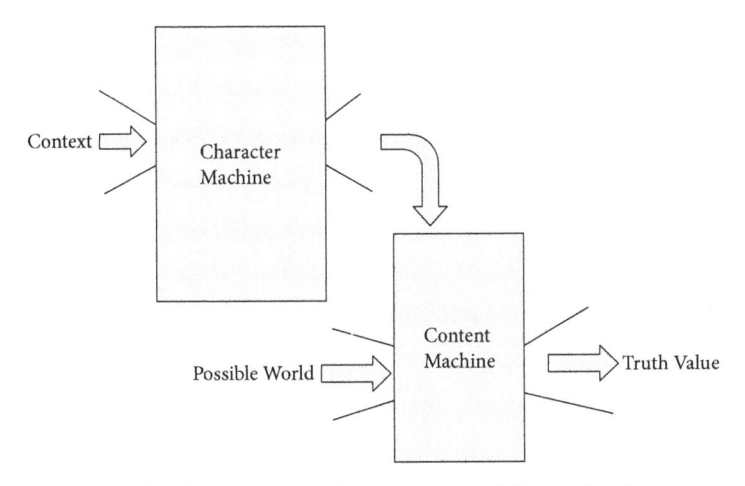

[Diagram: Context → Character Machine → (output) → Content Machine; Possible World → Content Machine → Truth Value]

Let's consider the content machine more carefully. In this diagram, we describe the content machine as asking for a possible world for input, and then producing a truth value as output. We know why we want a truth value as output: because our final goal is to be able to figure out whether linguistic contributions are true or false. But why do we need a possible world as input? We have by default inserted our earlier picture of possible worlds truth conditions, but it would be preferable to have a clear theoretical reason for adopting a particular account of Kaplanian contents.

Kaplan has a central argument, the Operator Argument, that drives the view that contents need possible worlds as inputs to determine truth values. But as we will see, the Operator Argument is a very powerful argument, and Kaplan in fact uses it to defend a view different from our earlier account of possible worlds truth conditions—instead, Kaplan argues that his contents need both *worlds* and *times* as inputs to determine truth values. We will then suggest that the Operator Argument is even more powerful than Kaplan realizes, and that followed through to its natural consequence, we get a picture of Kaplanian contents different from Kaplan's official view, and one that then leads us naturally into the alternative picture of Indexed Truth accounts.

Kaplan argues that the demands of a *compositional meaning theory* show us that we need truth relative to possible worlds to account for the contribution of words like *might* and *must* to truth values of sentences. Remember that one of the things we want from a theory of meaning is for it to show us how the meanings of complex expressions depend on the meanings of their component parts. In Chapter 4 we considered rules such as:

(Not Rule) The content of 'Not(S)' (as used in context C) is true if and only if the content of S (as used in context C) is not true.

(And Rule) The content of 'S1 and S2' (as used in context C) is true if and only if the content of S1 (as used in context C) is true and the content of S2 (as used in context C) is true.

(We have adjusted these rules slightly to fit into a two-stage character-and-content theory.) How can we give a rule of this form for sentences containing words like *might, must, possibly,* and *necessarily*? We want something like:

(Must Rule) The content of 'Must (S)' (as used in context C) is true if and only if the content of S (as used in context C) is . . . ???

But how do we fill in the question marks? It looks like what we want on the right-hand side is that the content of S is *true in every possible world*. But we can't say that unless contents are the kinds of things that are true or false *in worlds*, rather than just true or false *all by themselves*.

This is Kaplan's *Operator Argument*. It claims that contents require worlds as inputs (contents have 'world gaps') because we can sensibly modify contents with modal operators like *necessarily*.

What is an Operator?

We have already seen that sentences are true or false relative to different parameters. Sentences get truth values relative to times, relative to worlds, relative to places. An operator is a bit of language that combines with a sentence to make a more complicated sentence. The more complicated sentence gets its truth value by forcing the contained sentence to be checked for truth or falsity relative to a different parameter (different time, different world, and so on) than the main sentence uses.

Consider first the simple sentence 'Alex is happy'. This sentence gets truth values relative to times. Maybe it is true relative to Monday, and false relative to Tuesday. When uttered on Tuesday, it is its truth value relative to Tuesday that we care about.

(continued)

> *Continued*
>
> Now consider the complex sentence 'On Monday, Alex is happy'. This sentence is formed by taking the operator 'On Monday' and combining it with the sentence 'Alex is happy'. The operator 'On Monday' then forces the contained sentence 'Alex is happy' to be checked for truth or falsity specifically on Monday. So suppose we want to know whether 'On Monday, Alex is happy' is true or false relative to Tuesday. As we think our way through the sentence, we begin by thinking about truth relative to Tuesday. But when we encounter the operator 'On Monday', we shift to thinking about truth relative to Monday, and thus by the time we get to the contained sentence 'Alex is happy', we are thinking about Monday rather than Tuesday. Since Alex is happy on Monday, 'On Monday, Alex is happy' is true relative to Tuesday. (And, indeed, it is true relative to every time.)
>
> Other operators shift other parameters. The sentence 'It is raining' is true relative to some locations and false relative to others. The operator 'In St Andrews' is a location operator. It combines with 'It is raining' to form the complex sentence 'In St Andrews, it is raining'. In assessing that complex sentence for truth relative to a location, we shift, when we encounter the operator, to checking for truth in St Andrews. The truth of the sentence thus depends on whether it is raining specifically in St Andrews.
>
> Some operators are quantificational, because they don't specify a particular value for the shifted parameter, but rather tell us to consider a range of values. So 'Every Monday' is a quantificational time operator—when we combine it with 'Alex is happy', we get the complex sentence 'Every Monday, Alex is happy'. When we consider the truth value of that sentence at some particular time, the time operator then tells us to check the contained sentence for truth at *each* time that is a Monday.

If the Operator Argument works, it is a powerful argument. Kaplan (1977/1989) notes that it also supports the conclusion that contents give truth values only relative to a world *and a time*. Temporal operators can be added to sentences in the same way that modal operators can be. So for 'Yesterday, a giraffe was on the tarmac' to make sense, we need a *temporal gap* in the claim that a giraffe was on the tarmac for 'Yesterday' to fill. So 'A giraffe was on the tarmac' does not determine a truth value by itself, or even in combination with a world, but only together with a world and a time. This is what leads to Kaplan's official view that contents are functions from worlds *and times* to truth values.

But modal operators and temporal operators are not the only kinds of operators we find in natural languages. We can also use locational operators, as in 'In Chicago, a giraffe is on the tarmac'. We can use temperature operators, as in 'At temperatures above 212 degrees Farenheit, water boils'. We can apply vagueness-standards operators, as in 'Speaking loosely, France is hexagonal'. If we accept the Operator Argument, we must conclude that contents get truth values relative to worlds, times, locations, temperatures, vagueness standards, and many other parameters as well.

It starts to look as if *contents get truth value relative to* all of the same things that *characters determine contents relative to*. The world of utterance can affect the content that a character determines; contents get truth values relative to worlds. The time of utterance can affect the content that a character determines; contents get truth values relative to times. The place of utterance can affect the content that a character determines; contents get truth value relative to places. And so on. Since contexts do the work of providing all of these things (times, places, worlds, and so on), we might as well take content truth to be relativized to *contexts*, just as we take characters to be.

6.3 Indexed Truth Theories

The thought that contents determine truth relative to a context, rather than just relative to a world, leads to a slight revision in our picture of the Kaplan machinery:

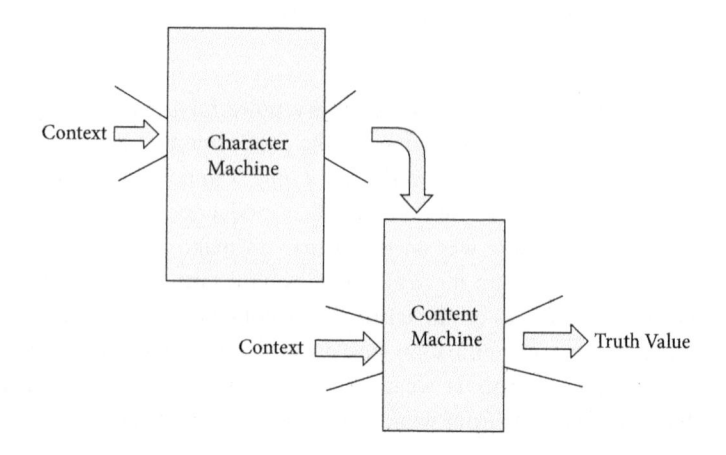

But once we draw the picture like this, it's natural to wonder why we need *two separate machines*. Why have one machine that takes context as input, and then produces *another* machine that *also* takes context as input? We could instead combine the two machines into one:

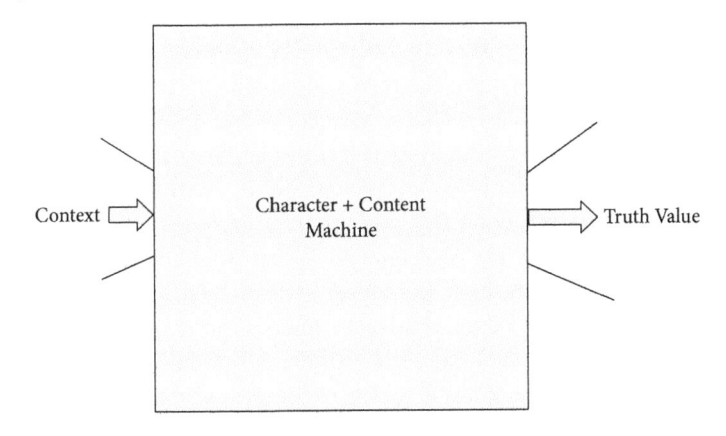

```
Context ⇒  [ Character + Content Machine ]  ⇒ Truth Value
```

David Lewis (1980) questions whether we *need* to adopt the two-machine picture. Lewis doesn't think it is *wrong* to have a two-machine picture—he just suggests that there is no interesting difference between it and the one-machine picture. Before we can determine whether there is an *interesting* difference, we need to make sure we're clear on the differences in the formal details of the one-machine and two-machine stories.

Imagine we find an ancient papyrus on which is written 'Alex is writing the exam she will give tomorrow'. Because we don't know when the papyrus was produced, we can't figure out whether what's written on it is true or false. Our ignorance of the relevant time shows up twice in our attempt to determine truth value. Because we don't know when the papyrus was written, we don't know what day is meant by 'tomorrow', and we don't know what time the present tense of 'is writing' picks out. Kaplan's picture locates those two pieces of ignorance in two different parts of the theory. On the two-stage theory, we *first* use a time to resolve what is meant by 'tomorrow', and thereby obtain a content such as *that Alex is writing the exam she will give on June 1*. And then *second*, that content is evaluated for truth or falsity relative to a time.

The Lewisian picture, on the other hand, denies that there is any interesting difference between or separation of the two pieces of ignorance. A sentence just gets a truth value relative to a time (among other things). The detailed story about how that truth value is calculated will appeal to that time more than once (it will get used both in interpreting the word 'tomorrow' and in interpreting the present tense), but the multiple appeals don't get located on different theoretical levels, or in different kinds of meaning like characters and contents.

Call this kind of theory an *Indexed Truth* theory. Indexed Truth theories take the basic form of a theory of meaning to be the assignment of truth values to sentences relative to *indices*, where indices are *whatever* bits of information we need to settle truth value. Our original toy theory of meaning in Chapter 4 was an Indexed Truth theory—one that made the additional assumption that the only kind of index we needed was possible worlds. The Lewisian thought is that what context sensitivity shows us is not that meaning comes on two levels, but rather that sentences get truth values relative to indices more complicated and more information-rich than just worlds. To avoid grappling with detailed questions about just *how* rich, we simply use contexts as indices, on the assumption that contexts are *whatever* settles all the kinds of dependencies. (Again, we haven't yet said anything about what contexts *really are*. We take up that question in the final part of the book. All that matters here is that contexts somehow or other determine parameters we need for evaluating sentences.)

The basic form of the Lewisian theory of meaning, then, is clauses of the form:

- Sentence S is true in context C if and only if . . .

Modal operators, for example, can have clauses like:

- 'Necessarily S' is true in context C if and only if S is true in every context C' that differs from C only in the world of the context.

The crucial difference between this approach and the Kaplanian approach is that we don't have separate levels of character and content. Context takes us straight from a sentence to a truth value. In the case of a more complicated sentence like our earlier 'Alex is writing the exam she will give tomorrow', Lewis' framework would allow for an analysis like:

- 'Alex is writing the exam she will give tomorrow' is true in context C iff there is an exam E such that (i) "Alex is writing E" is true in C and (ii) "Alex gives E" is true in C', where C' differs from C only in advancing the time of the context by one day although the fine details about how to produce such an analysis would still need to be worked out.

On a Kaplan-style two-stage theory, there is a deep theoretical difference among the following three examples:

1. Beth went to Paris yesterday and will go to Berlin tomorrow.
2. Alex is writing the exam she will give tomorrow.
3. Charlie is happy, and Denis is sad.

In the first example, we need a relevant time to evaluate both 'yesterday' and 'tomorrow', and that time is used in the transition from character to content. (We don't need *additional* times for the past and future tenses, because these will be past from the time of 'yesterday' and future from the time of 'tomorrow', respectively.) In the second example, as we've already seen, a relevant time is used once in the transition from character to content to evaluate 'tomorrow', and again in the transition from content to truth value to evaluate the present tense. In the third example, a relevant time is used twice to evaluate the two present-tense copulas, in both cases in the transition from content to truth value. But Lewis' claim is that there is not any interesting difference among the three cases.

Lewis doesn't feel the force of an interesting difference, and is thus attracted to an Indexed Truth account, on which all three sentences simply use the time of the index (= the context) to determine the truth value of the sentence. To get a better understanding of what indexed truth conditions sentences will have, we can use the following method:

Kaplan-To-Lewis Translation Method: Suppose for some sentence S we know the Kaplanian character and content of S. Then we can give the Lewisian indexed truth conditions for S:
- S is true relative to context C just in case the Kaplanian character of S determines in C some Kaplanian content CON, and CON is true relative to C.

For example, consider the sentence 'I am happy'. Suppose we want to know whether the indexed truth conditions for 'I am happy' make it true relative to a context C whose agent is Alex and whose time is June 1. Then we reason as follows:

1. 'I am happy' is true relative to C if and only if the Kaplanian character of 'I am happy' determines in C a Kaplanian content CON, and CON is true relative to C.
2. The Kaplanian character of 'I am happy' in context C determines the Kaplanian content *that Alex is happy*.
3. The Kaplanian content *that Alex is happy* is true relative to context C if and only if Alex is happy on June 1.
4. So, 'I am happy' is true relative to C if and only if Alex is happy on June 1.

6.4 Two Problems for Indexed Truth Accounts

The single-stage Indexed Truth account has the virtue of simplicity. But that very simplicity runs the risk of losing the philosophical payoffs we observed in the previous chapter for the two-stage theory. Recall that the Kaplan two-stage theory has the virtues of explaining Agreement and Disagreement, Rigidity, Kaplanian Logical Truths, and Cognitive Significance (see Chapter 5, Philosophical Payoffs of the Character–Content Distinction). An Indexed Truth account is well positioned to handle Kaplanian Logical Truths and Cognitive Significance. The sentence 'I am here now' will come out to be true relative to every index, because the index will provide values for 'I', 'here', and 'now' in a way that makes the sentence come out true. (Or will it? What if the person provided for 'I' isn't at the place provided for 'here'? This worry is connected to the worry about *propriety* of context that Kaplan's approach faces. We return to this topic in Chapter 8 when we discuss answering machine cases.) Similarly, Indexed Truth accounts deal well with Cognitive Significance, because such accounts give two occurrences of 'I am in danger' the same meaning (the same rule for deriving a truth value from a context), and occurrences of 'I am in danger' and 'You are in danger' different meanings.

But Indexed Truth accounts have more difficulty giving adequate treatments of Agreement and Disagreement and of Rigidity. The crucial observations behind Agreement and Disagreement can be summed up in two important types of data points:

Context-Sensitive Agreement: If Alex says 'I am happy', and Beth says to Alex 'You are happy', then they have thereby agreed.

INDEXED TRUTH ACCOUNTS 115

Lack of Context-Sensitive Agreement: If Alex and Beth both say 'I am happy', then they have not thereby agreed.

Lack of Context-Sensitive Agreement immediately shows that we cannot, once we include context sensitivity, capture agreement by sameness of Indexed Truth conditions. Suppose Alex and Beth both say 'I am happy'. Alex and Beth speak in two different contexts, First and Second, where First has Alex as speaker and Second has Beth as speaker. On Kaplan's account, the *one* sentence type then produces *two* contents. Relative to First, it produces the content *that Alex is happy*. Relative to Second, it produces the content *that Beth is happy*. But Lewis' account cuts out the middle man. On it, the one sentence type just has one indexed truth condition. (We can see what the indexed truth conditions are by using the Kaplan-to-Lewis Translation Method above.) If Alex is happy and Beth is not, then the single truth conditions determine that "I am happy" is true relative to First and false relative to Second. Both Alex's utterance and Beth's utterance have those truth conditions, so Alex and Beth say things with the same indexed truth conditions. But they do not agree, so sameness of indexed truth conditions does not suffice for agreement.

Context-Sensitive Agreement, on the other hand, shows that sameness of indexed truth conditions is not necessary for agreement. The sentence types 'I am happy' and 'You are happy' do not have the same indexed truth conditions. If Alex's context determines Beth as the audience, then 'I am happy' is true relative to it (because Alex is happy), but 'You are happy' is false relative to it (because Beth is not happy). So 'I am happy' and 'You are happy' don't have the same truth value relative to every context, and hence don't have the same indexed truth conditions. But Alex and Beth agree when Alex says 'I am happy' and Beth says 'You are happy', so sameness of indexed truth conditions cannot be necessary for agreement. Again, it is the missing middle man that was doing the work for Kaplan in explaining agreement and disagreement.

Call this the *Problem of Same-Saying*: how, without a separate level of Kaplanian content, can an Indexed Truth account explain when two utterances say the same thing?

Recall from Chapter 5 that there is a distinction between *rigid* and *nonrigid* context-sensitive expressions. Consider, for example, 'tomorrow' and 'the next day'. These are both context sensitive, and in simple cases they behave exactly alike. But in complex cases, their behavior comes apart. Consider the pair:

- Last Monday, you said that you would turn in your paper tomorrow.
- Last Monday, you said that you would turn in your paper the next day.

Spoken on Thursday, the first of these reports a commitment to turn in the paper on Friday, while the second of these reports a commitment to turn in the paper on Tuesday. 'Tomorrow' acts rigidly here—no matter what tense operators it is embedded under, it continues to refer to the day after the time of the context. 'The next day', on the other hand, acts nonrigidly. Unembedded, it also refers to the day after the time of the context, but under a tense operator like 'last Monday', it refers to the day after the time determined by the tense operator. If the tense operator is quantificational, then the referent of 'the next day' will vary with the varying value of the quantifier, while the referent of 'tomorrow' will remain stable:

- Every time I talk to you about your overdue assignment, you say that you will turn it in tomorrow.
- Every time I talk to you about your overdue assignment, you say that you will turn it in the next day.

The first of these reports a stable intention to turn in the assignment at a rapidly approaching specific future date; the second reports a goalpost-shifting intention in which the due date is constantly moved back.

In a Kaplan-style two-stage theory, we capture rigidity through the separation of character and content. 'Tomorrow' continues to pick out Friday (when spoken on Thursday) even when prefixed by 'Last Monday' because the *character* of 'tomorrow' tells us to put into *content* the day Friday (when spoken on Thursday). So the content of:

- Last Monday you said that you would turn in your paper tomorrow.

is the same as the content of:

- Last Monday you said that you would turn in your paper on Friday.

In a single-stage Indexed Truth account, however, we don't have separate levels of character and content, so we can't capture rigidity by placing it in character. All we do is take a time (and whatever other parameters are determined by the context) and use it to determine a truth value. There is no room to separate out the role of the time in the meaning of 'tomorrow' and in the meaning of 'the next day'. Call this the *Problem of Rigidity*: how, without using a separation between character and content, can we account for the rigidity of words like 'I', 'now', and 'tomorrow'?

All of this sounds like very bad news for Indexed Truth accounts, and could make us think we've gone down an unpromising path. Nothing we've said in this chapter *forced* us to switch from the Kaplan two-stage approach to the Indexed Truth one-stage approach. We could simply have accepted the full consequences of the Operator Argument and adopted a version of Kaplan's theory on which characters are functions from contexts to contents, and contents are functions from contexts to truth values. Then we could have retained Kaplan's two-stage accounts of rigidity and same-saying and avoided the current bad news. But in the next two chapters we will see that Indexed Truth accounts have responses available to the Problems of Same-Saying and Rigidity, and that these problems open up interesting new issues, and allow Indexed Truth accounts to fit into an overall theory of communication in ways importantly different from Kaplan's approach.

CENTRAL POINTS IN CHAPTER 6

- According to Kaplan's Operator Argument, if there are operators in the language that shift a parameter (as 'it used to be' shifts time, or 'might' shifts world), then sentences get truth values only relative to that parameter.
- Thorough application of the Operator Argument then suggests that sentences get truth values relative to contexts, with contexts then providing times, worlds, places, and so on.
- An Indexed Truth theory of meaning tells us the truth value of sentences relative to contexts. Unlike Kaplan's theory, it is not a two-stage theory, and has no separation of character and content.
- Indexed Truth conditions can be systematically extracted from a Kaplan-style theory.
- Indexed Truth theories are confronted with the Problem of Same-Saying and the Problem of Rigidity—two problems that Kaplan's approach does not face.

QUESTIONS FOR CHAPTER 6

Comprehension Questions

6.1. Construct Operator Arguments for three parameters not mentioned in the text.
6.2. Can you think of features of Kaplanian contexts that are not amenable to Operator Arguments?
6.3. Using the translation method, give Indexed Truth conditions for the following sentences:
   - You are happy.
   - I am taller than you.
   - You are taller than me.
   - It is raining here.
   - It is raining here now.

6.4. Give other examples, not involving 'I' or 'you', to show sameness of Indexed Truth conditions is neither necessary nor sufficient for agreement.
6.5. Devise an example like the 'last Monday' one in the text, not involving 'tomorrow' and 'the next day', which illustrates the point about rigidity.

Exploratory Questions

6.6. Cappelen and Hawthorne (2009) give a detailed presentation of Kaplan's Operator Argument, in which it uses three premises they call Parameter Dependence, Uniformity, and Vacuity:

   L1. *Parameter Dependence*: S is only evaluable for truth once a value along parameter M is specified.
   L2. *Uniformity*: S is of the same semantic type when it occurs alone or when it combines with E.
   L3. *Vacuity*: E is semantically vacuous (i.e., it doesn't affect truth value) when it combines with a sentence that semantically supplies a value for M.
   L4. E is not redundant when it combines with S.
   L5. By *Vacuity* and (L4), S does not supply a value for M when it combines with E.
   L6. By *Uniformity* and (L5), S does not supply a value for M when it occurs alone.
   L7. By *Parameter Dependence* and (L6), S can't be evaluated for truth. (71)

   Consider the prospects for resisting the Operator Argument by rejecting Vacuity. Vacuity claims that, for example, combining a temporal operator with a sentence that already contains a time specification is vacuous. Thus there can be, according to Vacuity, no difference in truth value between:

- John swam on July 6, 2011.
- In the past, John swam on July 6, 2011.
- On December 3, 2013, John swam on July 6, 2011.

But consider the following line of thought:

- 'It is raining' and 'It is raining now', both said in the same context, say the same thing.
- Speaking at time t_1, 'It is raining now' and 'It is raining at time t_1' say the same thing.
- 'It is raining' can be non-vacuously combined with 'at time t_2'.
- So 'It is raining at time t_1' can be non-vacuously combined with 'at time t_2'.
- So Vacuity is false.

Alternatively, we think the future is 'metaphysically open', in that the state of the world at any time t_1 is not yet settled at any earlier time t_2. Would this give us reason, speaking at t_1, to endorse 'It is raining at time t_1' but reject 'At time t_2, it is true that it is raining at time t_1'?

6.7. Cases similar to the ones just given contrasting 'tomorrow' with 'the next day' can be given using the modal term 'actual'. Compare:

- It could have been that everyone who is rich is poor.
- It could have been that everyone who is actually rich is poor.

The first claim is false, since it describes an incoherent possibility in which people are simultaneously rich and poor. But the second is true, because it describes the coherent possibility in which Bill Gates, Warren Buffet, and all the other people who in our world are rich, are instead poor.

But 'actual' doesn't always seem to behave in this way. Sometimes 'actual' doesn't seem to link back to our world, but rather stays with the world of evaluation, as in:

- If my mother were to be elected president, I'd be so excited to be actually related to the president!

In other cases, 'actual' looks like it links back not to our world, but to an 'intermediate' possibility, as in:

- Bill Gates is not only rich, but essentially rich, so that he couldn't possibly be poor. So it's not true that it could have been that everyone who is actually rich is poor, because Bill Gates is actually rich, and couldn't have been poor. But it might have been that Bill Gates was never born. And had Bill Gates never been born, then it would have been true that it could have been that everyone who is actually rich is poor.

Consider how we might give a theory of meaning for 'actually' that deals with this full range of data. Can we get similar cases for temporal terms like 'now', 'today', and 'tomorrow'?

FURTHER READING FOR CHAPTER 6

For more on Kaplan's Operator Argument, see Cappelen and Hawthorne (2009) and Glanzberg (2011).

For challenges to the thought that operators are the right model to use in thinking about tense, see Partee (1973) and Evans (1985).

For discussion of how an Indexed Truth theory would fit into an overall theory of language and communication, see King (2003) and Ninan (2010).

For resistance to the use of Indexed Truth values, see Soames (2011).

For an extended defense of the claim that propositions are true relative to times as well as worlds, see Brogaard (2012).

7

The Problem of Rigidity
Double Indexing and Monsters

7.1 Where We Are and the Plan for This Chapter

We have now seen two ways of giving a theory of meaning for context-sensitive language: a Kaplan-style two-stage character-and-content approach, and a one-stage Indexed Truth approach. At the end of the previous chapter we suggested that Indexed Truth accounts face two important problems that Kaplan's approach is immune to. First, the Problem of Same-Saying: Indexed Truth accounts don't produce a helpful notion of what is said by an utterance. Second, the Problem of Rigidity: Indexed Truth accounts don't explain why context sensitive expressions are rigid.

In this chapter, we focus on a formal device for fixing the second problem. The formal innovation is *double indexing*. Double indexing is a tricky technical notion, so we take some time carefully introducing it. Once we have a clear picture of double indexing, we will see that double indexing looks like a way of erasing the difference between Kaplanian and Indexed Truth accounts. Kaplan's theory can be thought of as a specific *kind* of double-indexed theory. What makes Kaplan's version of double-indexing distinctive, from this point of view, is that the character-content distinction builds in a ban on Kaplanian monsters. Other kinds of double-indexed accounts allow for the possibility of monsters. Choosing between a Kaplanian account and a double-indexed account thus requires determining whether there are, in fact, monsters. So we consider some strategies for responding to the apparently monstrous data we discussed in Chapter 5.

Double indexing, while fixing the Problem of Rigidity, at first glance seems to make the Problem of Same-Saying worse. In the next chapter we turn to this problem, showing that double indexing, despite first appearances, actually offers resources that help the Indexed Truth theorist address the Problem of Same-Saying.

We then close by observing that the question of whether there are monsters can be seen as a question about whether we can literally speak *from* a different time, world, or person, in the same way that we can literally speak *of* a different time, world, or person. Raising this question in turn raises questions about what contexts are, and what it is to be in a context, which we turn to in the third section of the book.

7.2 Fixing the Problem of Rigidity with Double Indexing

The Problem of Rigidity has two parts. First, there is a bit of data about languages:

1. Expressions like 'tomorrow', 'now', 'here', and 'I' are rigid, while 'the next day', 'the current time', 'the current location', and 'the speaker' are not rigid. So in some cases, replacing one of the rigid expressions with the corresponding nonrigid expression changes the truth value:
   - Last Monday, you said you would turn in your homework *tomorrow*.
   - Last Monday, you said you would turn in your homework *the next day*.
2. An Indexed Truth account assigns meanings to the rigid and nonrigid expressions in the same way. Both 'tomorrow' and 'the next day' are assigned the day after the time of the context; both 'here' and 'the current location' are assigned the place of the context.

The key to fixing this problem is to move to a *double-indexing* theory. Sentences get evaluated with respect to a *pair* of contexts: the Stable Context and the Shiftable Context. Some expressions (like 'tomorrow', 'now', 'here', and 'I') inherit their values from the Stable Context, and other expressions (like 'the next day', 'the current time', 'the current location', and 'the speaker') inherit their values from the Shiftable Context. Operators like tenses and modals can change the Shiftable Context, but not the Stable Context. The result will be that expressions getting values from the Stable Context will be rigid, because operators in the sentence will not affect their referent, while expressions getting values from the Shiftable Context will be nonrigid.

Let's unpack that key thought and see how it works. Suppose we have two contexts, Early and Late:

- Early: The time of Early is 1985.
- Late: The time of Late is 2015.

On the double-indexing approach, all expressions gets an extension relative to a *pair* of a Stable Context and a Shiftable Context. Consider the difference between 'now' and 'the current time'. Because 'now' is rigid, it gets its extension by looking only at the Stable Context. As a result:

- Relative to (Stable, Shiftable), 'the person who is president now' picks out whoever is president at the time of Stable.

So we get the following grid:

'The person who is president now'		Shiftable Context	
		Early	Late
Stable Context	Early	Reagan	Reagan
	Late	Obama	Obama

On the other hand, because 'the person who is president' (without the rigid 'now') is nonrigid, it gets its extension by looking only at the Shiftable Context:

- Relative to (Stable, Shiftable), 'the person who is president' picks out whoever is president at the time of Shiftable.

So we get a different grid:

'The person who is president'		Shiftable Context	
		Early	Late
Stable Context	Early	Reagan	Obama
	Late	Reagan	Obama

Suppose now that expressions like 'in 1985' change the Shiftable Context, but not the Stable Context:

- 'In 1985, the person who is president now was a Republican' is true relative to (Stable, Shiftable) just in the case that 'The person who is president now is a Democrat' is true relative to (Stable, Early).

'The person who is president now' picks out Obama relative to (Late, Early). So 'In 1985, the person who is president now was a Republican' is true only if *Obama* was a Republican in 1985. He wasn't, so the sentence is false.

On the other hand, 'the person who is president' picks out Reagan relative to (Late, Early). So 'In 1985, the person who was president was a Republican' is true only if *Reagan* was a Republican in 1985. He was, so the sentence is true. The double indexing thus allows us to capture the difference between rigid and nonrigid expressions.

7.3 Character, Content, and Double Indexing

Using double indexing allows an Indexed Truth account to capture the rigid–nonrigid distinction among context-sensitive expressions. A two-stage Kaplan theory can then be thought of as a special case of a double-indexed account. Recall our earlier picture of the doubled Kaplanian machinery:

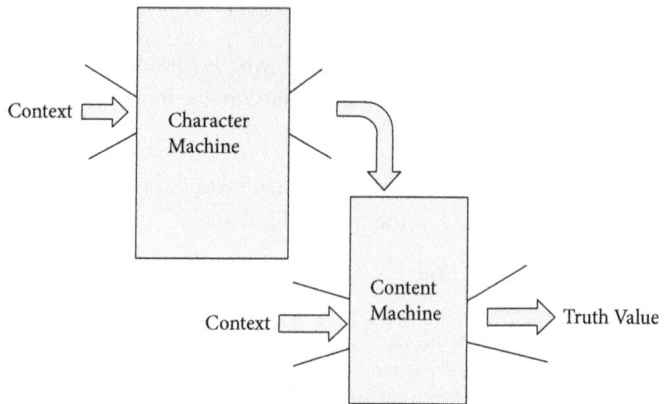

In the previous chapter we contrasted this picture with a single machine that took the context directly to a truth value. What we've seen here is that rigidity marks a real formal difference between the single and the double machine. The single machine only has one context as input. If operators in a sentence change any feature of that context, the original context is then lost. This is what makes rigidity difficult for simple Indexed Truth accounts. But double-indexed accounts have a crucially different picture of the machinery:

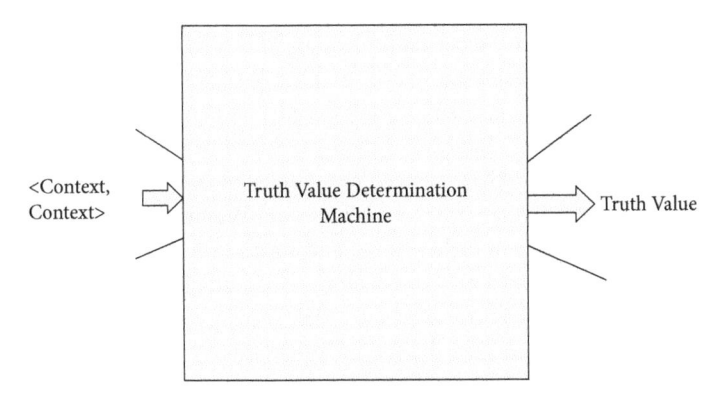

```
<Context, Context>  ⇒  [ Truth Value Determination Machine ]  ⇒  Truth Value
```

Here we have only a single machine, but the machine gets two contexts as input. But now the difference from the two-machine picture really is elusive. What does it matter whether we identify two machines, or bundle them together and call them a single machine, if the inputs and the outputs are the same in either case? In a double-indexed account, context is used twice in determining a truth value. Similarly, in a Kaplan theory, context is used twice in determining a truth value—once to get from character to content, and once to get from content to truth value. In Kaplan's terminology, the first use of context (corresponding to the Stable Context) is as the *context of utterance*, and the second use of the context (corresponding to the Shiftable Context) is as the *circumstance of evaluation*. The context of utterance does the job of determining what is said, and the circumstance of evaluation does the job of determining whether what is said is true or false.

To summarize: it initially looked like rigidity provided an argument *for* Kaplanian accounts and *against* Indexed Truth accounts. But double indexing gives a more sophisticated version of Indexed Truth accounts, and can account for rigidity. So at this point it looks like a tie. More than that, it looks like there may be no interesting difference between the two pictures. They start to look just like two ways of carving up the same underlying apparatus.

7.4 Are Monsters Evidence for Double Indexing?

But it turns out that we can find an interesting difference between the two ways of organizing our theory. On Kaplan's view, the circumstance of evaluation can be shifted, but the context of utterance cannot. Suppose a past-tense sentence 'Alex used to be happy' is uttered on Wednesday. The context of utterance provides the time Wednesday, which is then used to determine the content of what is said—namely, *that Alex is happy at a time before Wednesday*. We then need to determine whether that content is true. To do that, we need to provide the content with a time of evaluation. The starting time of evaluation is Wednesday, but the past tense shifts that time to earlier times, and we consider the truth value of 'Alex is happy' for various times before Wednesday. If there is a time before Wednesday relative to which 'Alex is happy' is true, then 'Alex used to be happy' is true as uttered on Wednesday.

But the double-indexed machinery as such does not *have* to restrict shifting in this way. We can easily write down definitions that shift the Stable Context (in Kaplan's terms, the context of utterance) instead, or that shift both indices. We could say, for example, that 'Super-Past S' is true relative to times t_1 and t_2 if there is a pair of times t_3 and t_4, with t_3 before t_1 and t_4 before t_2, such that S is true relative to t_3 and t_4. Of course, if we want to capture rigidity we shouldn't use double-shifting operators. But all that tells us is that normal temporal operators like *it used to be* or *last Wednesday* and normal modal operators like *necessarily* or *it might be* aren't double-shifting, because context-sensitive words like "I", "now", and "actually" are rigid with respect to them. It leaves open the possibility that there are other contexts in which rigidity fails.

Both the Kaplanian account and the double-indexed account are able to explain rigidity. However, they explain it in importantly different ways. Both accounts agree that there is a distinction between rigid and nonrigid context-sensitive expressions. According to Kaplan, this distinction tracks whether a context-sensitive expression has a character that determines its referent (that is, determines a rigid intension), or whether it has a character that determines a property, and then has that property fix a referent in a world (that is, determines a nonrigid intension). According to the double-indexed account, the rigid–nonrigid distinction tracks whether a context-sensitive expression has its referent settled by the first or second index in the doubled index of evaluation.

For Kaplan, rigidity is an absolute feature—because reference is settled in the transition from character to content, no operator can shift the reference of a rigid expression. But the double-indexed approach doesn't treat rigidity as absolute. *Normal* operators will treat words like 'I' and 'now' as rigid, but as we've just seen, the double-indexed account can allow for *nonstandard* operators that shift the first ('context of utterance') index.

If Kaplan is right that there are no monsters in natural language, then we have reason to prefer his account (which enforces a ban on monsters) to the general double-indexed account (which has no explanation for the absence of monsters). Let's compare how the Kaplan two-stage account and a double-indexing version of the Indexed Truth account would treat 'Never put off until tomorrow what you can do today'. Suppose this sentence is uttered in some context C, whose time is June 1.

1. On Kaplan's account, the character of 'Never put off until tomorrow what you can do today' combines with C to produce a content: *that one should never put off until June 2 what one can do on June 1*. (We'll ignore extra complications coming from the second-person pronoun 'you'.) That content then gets a truth value relative to a time. We have:
    - *That one should never put off until June 2 what one can do on June 1* is true at time t if there is no time t' at which it is true *that one should put off until June 2 what one can do on June 1*.

So 'Never put off until tomorrow what you can do today', as uttered in C, communicates that there is no time at which it's true that you should put off until June 2 what you can do on June 1. Kaplan's account thus doesn't give the right truth conditions.

2. On the double-indexed account, 'Never put off until tomorrow what you can do today' gets a truth value relative to a pair of times. 'Tomorrow' and 'today' get their referent from the first time index. Normally 'never' would shift only the second time index, but we can introduce a special monstrous 'never' that shifts both, so that 'Never S' is true relative to $\langle t_1, t_2 \rangle$ just in case there are no times $\langle t_3, t_4 \rangle$ relative to which S is true. So we get that 'Never put off until tomorrow what you can do today' is true relative to $\langle t_1, t_2 \rangle$ just in the case that there is no time t at which you should put off to t+1 what you can do at t. So the double-indexed account gives the right truth conditions.

Operators that shift the first index are monsters in the Kaplanian sense we discussed in Chapter 5. Recall that Kaplan holds that natural languages do not and cannot contain monsters. If that's right, we have reason to prefer Kaplan's theory to the double-indexed account, because Kaplan's theory explains why there are no monsters, while the double-indexed account would have to treat it as a lexical accident that there are none.

Of course, Kaplan's no-monsters claim doesn't look so good in light of the bad result his account gives for 'Never put off until tomorrow what you can do today'. But no single example will be decisive. Kaplan can always hold that there is something idiomatic or otherwise irregular about this example, so that 'tomorrow' and 'today' aren't functioning as *real* indexicals. We saw in Chapter 5, though, that there is a robust body of empirical evidence of apparently monstrous constructions. The dispute between Kaplan and the double-indexing Lewis thus depends on what we make of the evidence for monsters.

We are not trying in this chapter to answer definitively the question of whether there are monsters. Current linguistic and philosophical research remains divided on the significance of these constructions: on the empirical questions about what monster-like phenomena there are, on the formal question of how these phenomena are to be modeled, and on the theoretical question of what those modeling options tell us about context-sensitive language. We will close with two observations:

1. There are lessons to learn here about the methodology of philosophy of language. We have throughout this section been asking what shape a theory of meaning needs to have to deal well with context-sensitive language. Many of the considerations we have brought to bear on this question have been 'big picture' theoretical considerations about what the nature of communication is, how information is encoded in language and passed from one context to another, and how epistemological and cognitive features are tracked in context-sensitive language. But what the discussion of monsters shows is that these 'big picture' considerations can't be wholly divorced from detailed empirical questions about what sorts of constructions are available in the full range of human languages. The Kaplanian picture can give a philosophically satisfying integration of demands from psychology and logic, but still be vulnerable to novel data from speakers of Nez Perce. This

mixture of highly abstract considerations and detailed empirical data is one of the distinctive features of philosophy of language, especially as it has developed in recent decades.
2. Here is an uncontroversial, if remarkable, feature of human languages: we can use them to speak about times, places, and worlds far removed from us. If you say 'It could have been that Aristotle lived in Rome at the time of Augustus Caesar', you talk effortlessly about distant lands (if you aren't in Italy), the distant past, and a possible world other than our own. We can think of monsters as opening up the possibility that we can not only speak *about* distant times, places, and worlds, but actually literally speak *from* them. Monsters offer a vivid form of parasitism, in which we shift the context so that we temporarily speak from a different context. But the idea that we can with the right choice of words speak from a different context points to questions about what it is to be *in a context*. Language is a remarkable instrument, but not so remarkable that we can simply through the right choice of words literally come to be in different times and places. So if being in a context is a form of being in a place or a time, then it is too much to ask that monsters let us speak from different contexts. But perhaps being in a context is not so easily assimilated to being in a place or time. We turn to questions of this sort in the next chapter.

CENTRAL POINTS IN CHAPTER 7

- Without a character–content distinction, Indexed Truth approaches lack tools for explaining the rigidity of context-sensitive expressions.
- Rigidity can be recaptured in an Indexed Truth framework by using double indexing. In double indexing, sentences get truth values relative to pairs of indices. One index is shifted by operators in the sentence; the other is not.
- Formally, an Indexed Truth account with double indexing and a Kaplanian two-stage account are close to notational variants. There is a concern about whether there are really two competing theories here.
- But double indexing makes it straightforward to introduce monsters into a language. The empirical question of whether there are monsters thus becomes crucial for selecting our formal framework.
- The Kaplanian account has resources for resisting the evidence of monsters by giving an alternative explanation in terms of covert quotation.

QUESTIONS FOR CHAPTER 7

Comprehension Questions

7.1. Explain in your own words the problem for Indexed Truth theories posed by rigidity.

7.2. According to the double-indexing theory, some expressions receive their value from the Stable Context index, while others receive their value from the Shiftable Context index. Determine for each of the following context-sensitive expressions which context index it receives its value from:

> I, we, you, he, they, last year, recently, contemporary, actually, might, local, the tallest man now in the room, the tallest man in the room, before you arrived, every philosopher, too many giraffes, might

Then consider hypotheses about the distribution of rigid (stable-context) and nonrigid (shiftable-context) expressions.

7.3. Draw grids like those in the text for 'In 1985, the person who is president (/now) was Republican' for:

- In Rome, the weather here is a source of constant amusement

Exploratory Questions

7.4. Define a temporal operator 'On Super-Tuesday' as follows:

- 'On Super-Tuesday, S' is true relative to times t_1 and t_2 just in case S is true with respect to times t_3 and t_4, where t_3 and t_4 are the first Tuesdays before t_1 and t_2, respectively.

Consider the two sentences:

- On Super-Tuesday, you said you would give me the homework tomorrow.
- On Super-Tuesday, you said you would give me the homework the next day.

Are these two sentences equivalent? Why or why not?

7.5. Define another temporal operator 'On Wacky-Wednesday' so that:

- On Wacky-Wednesday you said you would give me the homework tomorrow.

is equivalent to:

- On Wednesday, you said you would give me the homework the next day.

and:

- On Wacky-Wednesday, you said you would give me the homework the next day.

is equivalent to:

- On Wednesday, you said you would give me the homework tomorrow.

7.6. In Chapter 5, we noted that 'said that' acts like a monster in Amharic, so that 'Jill said that I am a hero' can mean that Jill said of herself that she was a hero. But without going to cross-linguistic data, everyone agreed that quotation marks had a similar result. 'Jill said, "I am a hero"' means that Jill says of herself that she is a hero.

Consider whether Kaplan can use this observation as a strategy for defending against apparently monstrous constructions by treating them as secretly quotational. Show that constructions that are non-uniformly monstrous, such as free indirect discourse, present a challenge to this strategy, and consider whether there are good responses to that challenge. Should the quotational strategy be taken to show that there is no interesting problem of monsters, or to show that monsters are even more widespread than we initially thought, because quotation marks are monsters?

7.7. Discuss the relation between monsters and nonrigid context-sensitive expressions. What is wrong with the following line of thought?
   1. What is distinctive about monsters is that they cause context-sensitive language to be evaluated relative to contexts other than the actual context. So in Amharic 'Naomi said that I am a hero', 'I' gets evaluated relative to a context in which the actual speaker is replaced by Naomi.
   2. What is characteristic about nonrigid context-sensitive expressions is that they can be caused to be evaluated in contexts other than the actual context by operators in the sentence.
   3. So in 'On Monday you said you would turn in the paper the next day', the operator 'On Monday' causes 'the next day' to be evaluated in a context in which the time of utterance is replaced by Monday.
   4. So monsters are just expressions that cause context-sensitive expressions to do what nonrigid context-sensitive expressions do.

   Since Kaplan's framework can allow nonrigid context-sensitive expressions, it can allow monsters.

7.8. Above we distinguish between direct speech reports, in which what was said is reported verbatim using quotation, and indirect speech reports, in which there is no verbatim reporting requirement. But this distinction ignores certain intermediate cases, which employ the technique of mixed quotation. Consider this example:

1. Quine said that quotation has a 'certain anomalous feature'.

In this speech report, we report verbatim some but not all of the words that Quine used in speaking.

Consider whether mixed quotation can allow us to give a more satisfactory treatment of the monster data using quotational methods.

> **FURTHER READING FOR CHAPTER 7**

The original introduction of double indexing is in Kamp (1971). The formal tools of double indexing were given additional philosophical significance in Davies and Humberstone (1980), and became the basis for the important tradition of two-dimensional semantic. See Schroeter (2012) for an overview of two-dimensionalism.

For discussion of whether quotation can be used to avoid Kaplanian monsters, see Maier (2014).

For the suggestion that quotation is itself a context-shifting operator, see Recanati (2001).

For a general introduction to philosophical issues surrounding quotation, see Cappelen and Lepore (2012).

8

The Problem of Same-Saying

Two Strategies

8.1 Where We Are and the Plan for This Chapter

In the previous chapter we showed how an Indexed Truth theory can use double indexing to address the Problem of Rigidity. With double indexing, Indexed Truth theories can accommodate *monsters*, so if there are monsters in human languages, the Indexed Truth theories end up with a better account of rigidity than does Kaplan's theory. But there remains the Problem of Same-Saying. Even the simple versions of Indexed Truth theories face this problem. As we noted before, Indexed Truth accounts will say that two utterances of 'I am happy' by Alex and Beth have the same *Indexed Truth conditions*, while an utterance of 'I am happy' by Alex and an utterance of 'You are happy' by Beth have different Indexed Truth conditions. This fits poorly with the fact that in the first case, Alex and Beth say different things and don't agree with one another, while in the second case, Alex and Beth say the same thing and do agree with one another.

Adding double indexing into the mix doesn't fix this problem. So Indexed Truth theories remain at a serious explanatory disadvantage to Kaplan's account. In this chapter we consider two strategies for responding to the Problem of Same-Saying. The first strategy, which we associate with Lewis, responds by challenging the supposed data. Lewis is a *same-saying skeptic*: he denies that there are clear and stable facts about when speakers agree and disagree. Without such clear and stable facts, the Same-Saying challenge to the Indexed Truth theory simply cannot be mounted. Engaging with Lewis' same-saying skepticism helps raise important questions about what communication is, and connects back to discussions of minimalism and pluralism from Chapter 3.

The second strategy, which we associate with Stalnaker, is more conciliatory. Stalnaker develops a view that explains how double-indexed truth conditions for sentences can give rise to *informational* effects for speakers that can be characterized in simpler possible worlds terms. Stalnaker's account will produce the result that, although two utterances of 'I am happy' by different speakers have the same double-indexed truth conditions, they nevertheless cause audiences to update their beliefs about the world in different ways. At this 'update level', we thus have a response to the Problem of Same-Saying. We then close by noting cases in which Stalnaker's approach may in fact do *better* than Kaplan's, by giving a better account of how certain context-sensitive identity claims are informative.

8.2 Lewis' Same-Saying Skepticism

An Indexed Truth theorist can challenge the supposed data about the patterns of agreement and disagreement. Lewis (1980: 97) simply disagrees that the way we use talk of what is said has the features described above. Lewis starts by describing Kaplan's view on when the same thing is said:

Consider some further examples. (1) I say 'I am hungry'. You simultaneously say to me 'You are hungry'. What is said is the same. (2) I say 'I am hungry'. You simultaneously say 'I am hungry'. What is said is not the same. Perhaps what I said is true but what you said isn't. (3) I say on 6 June 1977 'Today is Monday'. You say on 7 June 1977 'Yesterday was Monday'. What is said is the same.... (5) I say on 6 June 1977 'It is Monday'. I might have said, in the very same context, '6 June 1977 is Monday', or perhaps 'Today is Monday'. What is said is not the same. What I did say is false on six days out of every seven, whereas the two things I might have said are never false.

Lewis then objects to that characterization:

I put it to you that not one of these examples carries conviction. In every case, the proper naive response is that in some sense what is said is the same for both sentence-context pairs, whereas in another—equally legitimate—sense, what is said is not the same. Unless we give it some special technical meaning, the locution 'what is said' is very far from univocal. It can mean the propositional content.... It can mean the exact words. I suspect that it can mean almost anything in between. (97)

Lewis observes that an Indexed Truth account can produce *multiple patterns* of similarity and difference among utterances. Consider again the case in which Alex says 'I am happy', and Beth says 'You are happy'. As we have already seen, Alex's utterance and Beth's utterance have different Indexed Truth conditions. Relative to a context in which happy Alex is the speaker and unhappy Beth is the audience, Alex's utterance is true and Beth's utterance is false. But of course Beth's utterance is not made in such a context, but rather in a context in which happy Alex is the audience. And an Indexed Truth account can use this fact to identify a pattern of *sameness* in Indexed Truth conditions.

Let's simplify by taking contexts to do nothing but specify speaker, audience, and world. We'll consider four worlds:

- Happy-Happy: Alex and Beth are both happy.
- Happy-Sad: Alex is happy and Beth is unhappy.
- Sad-Happy: Alex is unhappy and Beth is happy.
- Sad-Sad: Alex and Beth are both unhappy.

We can then consider eight different contexts. Each context will have one of Alex and Beth as speaker and the other of them as audience, and will have one of the above worlds as its world. We'll specify contexts by indicating the speaker and the world of the context. C(Alex,Sad-Happy), for example, will be the context having Alex as speaker, Beth as audience, and Sad-Happy as world.

We then get the following Indexed Truth conditions:

Context	'I am happy'	'You are happy'
C(Alex,Happy-Happy)	True	True
C(Alex,Happy-Sad)	True	False
C(Alex,Sad-Happy)	False	True
C(Alex,Sad-Sad)	False	False
C(Beth,Happy-Happy)	True	True
C(Beth,Happy-Sad)	False	True
C(Beth,Sad-Happy)	True	False
C(Beth,Sad-Sad)	False	False

As we expected, we find that 'I am happy' and 'You are happy' do not have the same Indexed Truth conditions. But given an utterance of 'I am happy' in a particular context, we can define the *worldly truth conditions* of that utterance as being all worlds which, when substituted for the world of the context, make 'I am happy' true. Alex's utterance of 'I am happy' is in context C(Alex,Happy-Sad). Putting Happy-Happy or Happy-Sad into the world position of this context makes 'I am happy' true, while putting in Sad-Happy or Sad-Sad makes 'I am happy' false. So the worldly truth conditions of Alex's utterance is the set {Happy-Happy, Happy-Sad}.

Beth's utterance of 'You are happy', on the other hand, is in context C (Beth,Happy-Sad). Putting Happy-Happy or Happy-Sad into the world position of that context makes 'You are happy' true, while putting either Sad-Happy or Sad-Happy in the world position makes 'You are happy' false. So Beth's utterance also has worldly truth conditions of {Happy-Happy, Happy-Sad}. The *sameness* in Alex's utterance and Beth's utterance, then, is not in their Indexed Truth conditions, but rather in their worldly truth conditions.

So Alex's and Beth's utterances are the same in one way (in their worldly truth conditions) and different in another way (in their Indexed Truth conditions). The strategy is to recognize that Indexed Truth conditions are very sensitive and fine-grained things—they capture variation with respect to many different parameters (speaker, audience, world, time, and so on). So Indexed Truth conditions of utterances very easily differ. But we can spot other patterns of similarity by *disregarding* some of that sensitivity, and considering variability only along some parameters.

But then what kind of sameness is the *right* kind of sameness for our talk of agreement and disagreement? Is what is said distinguished, for example, by full indexed truth conditions, or by worldly truth conditions, or by some other pattern discernible in the formal machinery given by an Indexed Truth account? Lewis' suggestion is that we should be skeptical about the robustness of the data about what is said. This data should emerge from patterns of agreement and disagreement, of saying the same and saying differently. Resolving the Problem of Same-Saying then requires finding some aspect of the meanings delivered by our theories to account for those patterns. Lewis suggests, however, that no single dominant pattern emerges from the data. For some purposes it is right to say that Alex and Beth agree; for other purposes it is wrong to say that they agree.

One of the important reasons to pursue the (often messy and complicated details of) formal theories of meaning is that they give us tools for making more precise and examining more carefully ideas that emerge elsewhere in our theorizing about language. Lewis' *same-saying skepticism*, for example, can be thought of as fitting in with the puzzles about shared content discussed in Chapters 2 and 3. We might think of Lewis as a kind of Pluralist (see section 3.4). Like Pluralists, he gives up the idea that there is any *one unique thing* that is what is said by an utterance of a context-sensitive sentence. Lewis observes that an Indexed Truth account naturally produces resources for giving multiple answers to whether two sentences (uttered in different contexts) say the same thing. Each sentence is associated with a rule for determining truth values in contexts. Sameness of what is said can be anything from perfect identity of the two rules to agreement of the rules on what truth value is determined in a particular context, with other varying degrees of agreement between these two extremes. But consider two other ways in which an Indexed Truth account can be pressed into the service of some of the options considered in Chapter 3:

1. Indexed Truth accounts can be seen as giving a formal picture friendly to Relativist-Minimalism (see section 3.4.6). The indexed truth conditions give a *minimal content* expressed by 'I am happy'. The key thought here is that indexed truth conditions are entirely cross-contextually portable. The sentence 'I am happy' has the indexed truth conditions it does completely independently of what context that sentence is used in. The formal price we pay for that portability is then the relativization of truth to contextual parameters—the minimal content shared by all utterances of 'I am happy' is, on this picture, not true or false in itself, but only true or false relative to various indices of the sort that context delivers.
2. Or we could think of the Indexed Truth account as giving the tools for developing a Radical Contextualist account (see section 1.3). The key thought here is that the various less fine-grained patterns of similarity that we can extract from indexed truth conditions are *not* entirely cross-contextually portable. Alex's utterance of 'I am happy' in C(Alex, Happy-Sad) and Beth's utterance of 'You are happy' in C(Beth, Happy-Sad) share the same worldly truth

conditions not because the sentences 'I am happy' and 'You are happy' *in general* share the same worldly truth conditions—we need the contextual setting to get the sameness of worldly truth conditions. The more we want to coarse-grain the indexed truth conditions, the more dependent on contextual setting the patterns of similarity will become. In the limit, we'll reach kinds of content that are difficult or impossible to share from one context to another.

The Problem of Same-Saying originally purported to be a point of superiority of the two-stage Kaplan theory over the single-stage Indexed Truth account. But the line of thought developed by the propositional skeptic shows that determining whether there is a *real* Problem of Same-Saying requires determining how we should address the problems of shared content. So long as those problems remain live, the Kaplan account will not be able to gain a decisive advantage over the Indexed Truth account.

8.3 Stalnaker and Contextual Subjectivism

One aspect of Kaplan's theory of context sensitivity is that character determines content via whatever the context *actually is*. A consequence of this is that if we don't know what context we are in, we don't know what contents we are expressing with our claims. If Alex has lost track of where she is, and doesn't know whether she is in St Andrews or Oslo, then when she says 'It is raining here', she doesn't know whether she says that it is raining in St Andrews or that it is raining in Oslo. And if she thinks to herself, 'It is raining here', she doesn't know whether she is *thinking* that it is raining in St Andrews or that it is raining in Oslo. Kaplan's theory thus results in what is called *content externalism*: the view that we don't always know what we are thinking and saying, and that what we are thinking and saying isn't fully determined by what's in our heads. Content externalism has been the focus of a vast philosophical literature over the last 40 years.

But we can develop a variation of Kaplan's view on which what matters is not what the context *objectively is*, but rather what we *subjectively take the context to be*. The simplest version of Subjective Contextualism would hold that if Alex thinks she is in Oslo, but is in fact in St Andrews, then when she says 'It is raining here', she says that it is raining in Oslo, rather than that it is raining in St Andrews. But this simplest version is implausible. If it is raining in St Andrews but not in Oslo, then Alex says something true when she says 'It is raining here', even if she is confused about where she is. But that means she does *not* say that it is raining in Oslo, since that is false.

To get an interesting version of Subjective Contextualism, we need to look at cases in which the speaker has multiple candidates for what context they are in. Return to the case in which Alex doesn't know whether she is in St Andrews or in Oslo. Then we want a sense in which she says *both* that it is raining in Oslo and that it is raining in St Andrews. To spell out that sense, we need to say more about what the conversational effects of an utterance are. At least in simple cases, the goal of a conversation is for people to share information about the world, and thereby reduce their collective ignorance. What they know about the world can be modeled in two equivalent ways:

1. As a list of facts known.
2. As a set of possible worlds that for all they collectively know, might be the actual world.

Suppose the conversation among Alex, Beth, and Charles has established that Alex is happy, that Beth is sad, and that Charles is hungry. Then we can represent their collective information about the world using possible worlds:

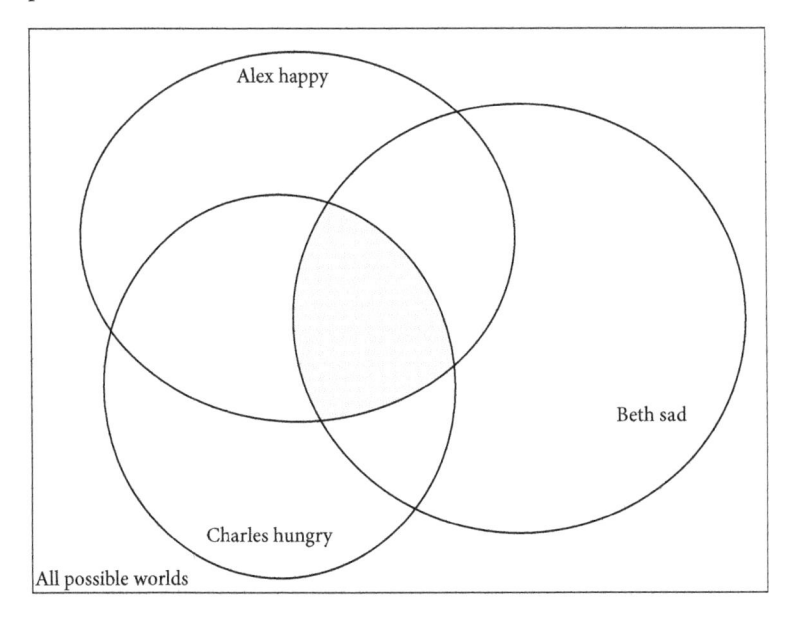

Alex, Beth, and Charles have succeeded in determining that the actual world is one of the worlds in the gray region that is the intersection of the happy Alex worlds, the sad Beth worlds, and the hungry Charles worlds. If Beth now says 'Alex is hungry', this new piece of information will further restrict the worlds that might be actual, thereby reducing their ignorance about where in possible space they are:

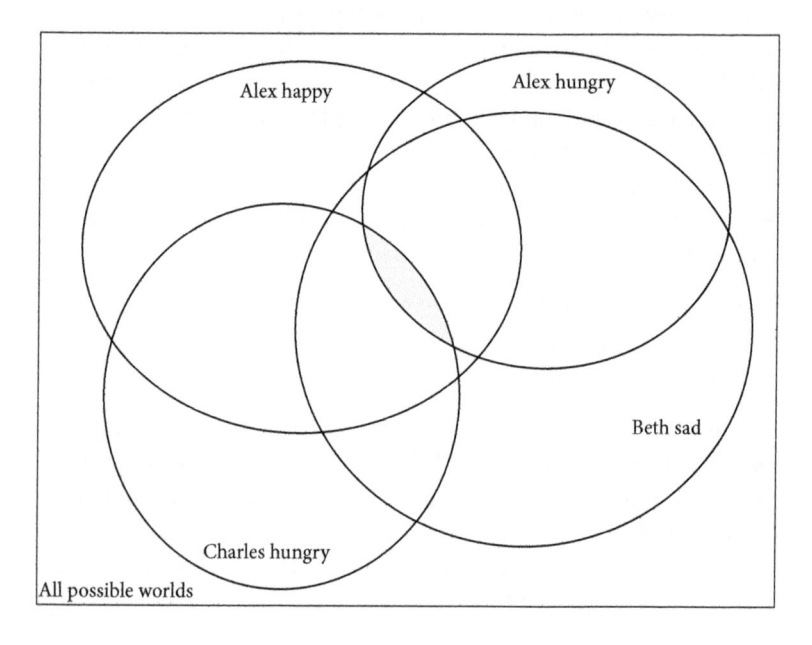

When we add context sensitivity to the picture, we discover that there are two kinds of ignorance that can afflict conversational participants. There can be *worldly* ignorance, which is the ignorance about which world is actual that we have been discussing. But there can also be *contextual* ignorance, which is ignorance about what context the conversation is taking place in.

Suppose Alex doesn't know whether she is in St Andrews or Oslo, and she doesn't know what the weather is like in either city. Then her worldly ignorance can be modeled by saying that she could be in any of four possible worlds:

1. Wet-Wet: It is raining in both St Andrews and Oslo.
2. Wet-Dry: It is raining in St Andrews but not raining in Oslo.

3. Dry-Wet: It is not raining in St Andrews but is raining in Oslo.
4. Dry-Dry: It is not raining in either St Andrews or Oslo.

Her *contextual* ignorance can be modeled by saying that she could be in one of two contexts:

1. StA: A context determining a location of St Andrews.
2. Oslo: A context determining a location of Oslo.

Since she doesn't know either which world she is in or what context she is in, there are eight possibilities for 'where she is', represented by ordered pairs of worlds and contexts:

| Wet-Wet, StA | Wet-Dry, StA | Dry-Wet, StA | Dry-Dry, StA |
| Wet-Wet, Oslo | Wet-Dry, Oslo | Dry-Wet, Oslo | Dry-Dry, Oslo |

Context-insensitive statements then reduce Alex's ignorance by eliminating columns of this table. If Alex hears an utterance 'It is raining in Oslo', she can eliminate the second and fourth column. But context-sensitive statements reduce Alex's ignorance in a more complicated way. Suppose instead that Alex hears Beth (looking out the window) say, 'It is raining here'. Alex still doesn't know what context she is in, so she doesn't know where it is raining. She thus doesn't get any specific worldly information, and can't directly eliminate any of the four possible worlds. She also can't eliminate either of the two candidate contexts. But she can eliminate some combinations of worlds and contexts. She knows, for example, that it's not the case that she is in an Oslo context and it is dry in Oslo. Her new state of ignorance is thus represented by:

| Wet-Wet, StA | Wet-Dry, StA | ~~Dry-Wet, StA~~ | ~~Dry-Dry, StA~~ |
| Wet-Wet, Oslo | ~~Wet-Dry, Oslo~~ | Dry-Wet, Oslo | ~~Dry-Dry, Oslo~~ |

And at this point she can conclude that she is not in the world Dry-Dry, because all combinations of it with any context have been eliminated.

8.4 Stalnaker, Updates, and Diagonals

This is the heart of Stalnaker's subjectivist version of a theory of meaning for context sensitivity. Context-sensitive utterances depend for their truth both on how the world is and on what the context of utterance was, so such utterances can be used to reduce our uncertainty on both fronts. In this section we will consider some more complicated examples of Stalnaker's approach to show the full extent of its versatility.

Stalnaker's theory is a version of a double-indexed theory, since sentences get truth values relative to pairs of worlds and contexts. So like Lewis, Stalnaker faces the Problem of Same-Saying. Two different utterances of 'I am happy' by two different people will have the same itndexed truth conditions, and Alex's utterance of 'I am happy' will have different indexed ruth conditions from Beth's utterance to Alex of 'You are happy'. Neither of these is the right result.

However, unlike Lewis, Stalnaker is not a same-saying skeptic. Stalnaker's goal is to agree with our Chapter 4 toy theory that what is said is just an intension, or a set of possible worlds. Achieving that goal involves two central ideas. First, we treat contextual ignorance as just a special form of worldly ignorance. Alex doesn't know the weather in St Andrews or Oslo, and she also doesn't know whether she is in a St Andrews-determining context or an Oslo-determining context. But her ignorance about what *context* she is in looks like it's just ignorance about where *she* is. If she had another piece of worldly information—for example, that Alex is in St Andrews—she would know what context she was in. So perhaps there are just three factual questions Alex doesn't know the answer to:

- Whether it is raining in St Andrews, whether it is raining in Oslo, and whether Alex is in St Andrews or Oslo.

We could then consider *eight* possible worlds: WWS, the world in which it is wet in St Andrews, wet in Oslo, and Alex is in St Andrews, and so on. If we knew which of those worlds Alex was in, we would thereby know the context she was speaking in. Contexts are just features of the world, so knowing all about the world entails knowing about the context. The following chart then gives the truth value of 'It is raining here' relative to all pairs of those worlds:

THE PROBLEM OF SAME-SAYING   143

	WWS	WWO	WDS	WDO	DWS	DWO	DDS	DDO
WWS	true	true	true	true	false	false	false	false
WWO	true	true	false	false	true	true	false	false
WDS	true	true	true	true	false	false	false	false
WDO	true	true	false	false	true	true	false	false
DWS	true	true	true	true	false	false	false	false
DWO	true	true	false	false	true	true	false	false
DDS	true	true	true	true	false	false	false	false
DDO	true	true	false	false	true	true	false	false

← Assessment world

↑ Context world

The world on the vertical axis indicates an option for what world Alex is speaking in (the context), and the world on the horizontal axis indicates an option for the world in which we are assessing the truth value of what she says. So, for example, if we take Alex to be speaking in the world DWS, she is speaking in St Andrews, and thus is saying of St Andrews that it is raining there. What she says is then false of the world DDO, because it is not raining in St Andrews in that world.

Second, we need to get from these two-dimensional charts to a simple intension to count as what is said. Stalnaker offers two strategies. First, in many cases we won't be subject to contextual ignorance. If Alex knows she is in Oslo, then we don't need to include the worlds WWS, WDS, DWS, and DDS. We are then left with the following portion of the chart:

	WWO	WDO	DWO	DDO
WWO	true	false	true	false
WDO	true	false	true	false
DWO	true	false	true	false
DDO	true	false	true	false

But now each of the four rows of the chart has the same list of truth values. So we can take the intension of Alex's utterance to be given by that row—what Alex says is true in WWO and DWO, and false in WDO and DDO. Alex's saying 'It is raining here' will then further reduce the ignorance of the conversation, so that the options for which world the conversation is in shifts from {WWO, WDO, DWO, DDO} to {WWO, DWO}. Any time there is no contextual ignorance, all the rows of the two-dimensional chart will be the same, and we can take what is said to be the intension given by those rows. That intension will then match the content assigned in Kaplan's theory.

However, if there is contextual ignorance, then the rows of the table will not have the same truth values. Since the rows are not the same, there is no unique candidate for the intension of the utterance. What are audience members supposed to do with utterances in such cases? Suppose Alex says 'It is raining here' in a case in which she doesn't know whether she is in St Andrews or in Oslo. Should the world WDO remain a live option for the conversational participants after this? If Alex is in a St Andrews context (for example, the first row), then WDO is not ruled out, but if she is in an Oslo context (for example, the second row), it is. When rows of the table differ, we don't know which worlds to keep and which to eliminate.

But there is a less direct procedure for updating the conversation. If the conversation is taking place in WDO, then Alex is in Oslo. And if Alex is in Oslo, then she says that it is raining in Oslo when she utters 'It is raining here'. But in WDO, it is *not* raining in Oslo. So (assuming Alex is reliable), WDO can be ruled out as a candidate world.

The crucial fact is that 'It is raining here', considered as uttered in WDO, is false when evaluated with respect to WDO. A world should be eliminated if the utterance is false with respect to the pair of that world with itself. We thus need to consider the *diagonal* of the chart:

	WWS	WWO	WDS	WDO	DWS	DWO	DDS	DDO
WWS	TRUE	true	true	true	false	false	false	false
WWO	true	TRUE	false	false	true	true	false	false
WDS	true	true	TRUE	true	false	false	false	false
WDO	true	true	false	FALSE	true	true	false	false
DWS	true	true	true	true	FALSE	false	false	false
DWO	true	true	false	false	true	TRUE	false	false
DDS	true	true	true	true	false	false	FALSE	false
DDO	true	true	false	false	true	true	false	FALSE

Alex's utterance eliminates as options all the worlds that produce a false entry along the diagonal. So WDO, DWS, DDS, and DDO are eliminated as options, and after Alex's utterance, the conversational participants know that they are in one of WWS, WWO, WDS, or DWO. They have thus learned that either they are in a rainy St Andrews or they are in a rainy Oslo.

Stalnaker's aspiration, then, is to give a theory that uses double indexing as a central component, but remains close to our starting toy theory by still associating each utterance with a set of worlds by considering the update effects of that utterance—the associated set of worlds is the set of worlds that are not eliminated from the conversational knowledge model by that utterance.

We will close our discussion of Stalnaker's contextual subjectivism by discussing an advantage it can claim over Kaplan's theory. Suppose Alex comes across someone who looks vaguely familiar, but whom she cannot place. The other person then tells her, 'I am Edward'. This utterance is *informative* for Alex. Upon hearing it, she goes from not knowing who she is talking to, to knowing. But for Kaplan, the informative nature of the utterance is puzzling. Since 'I am Edward' is uttered by Edward, the character of the sentence combined with the context of utterance determines Edward as the referent of 'I', and hence tells us that the content of Edward's utterance is *that Edward is Edward*. But learning that Edward is Edward isn't informative for Alex. She already knew that, so learning it can't explain how she now knows who she is talking to.

Consider how Stalnaker will analyze Edward's utterance. Let's assume that in the conversation, there is uncertainty about who the speaker is: it might be Edward, it might be Frank, and it might be George. (Of course, *Edward* knows who the speaker is, but the conversational uncertainty is a measure of what is uncertain to the conversational participants collectively.) So there are three relevant worlds:

1. The E world, in which Edward is the speaker.
2. The F world, in which Frank is the speaker.
3. The G world, in which George is the speaker.

We can then set out a two-dimensional chart for 'I am Edward' using these three worlds:

'I am Edward'	E world	F world	G world
E world	true	true	true
F world	false	false	false
G world	false	false	false

If the context is an Edward-context, then 'I am Edward' expresses the claim that Edward is Edward, which is then true in every possible world. If the context is a Frank-context, then 'I am Edward' expresses the claim that Frank is Edward, which is false in every possible world. And if the context is a George-context, then 'I am Edward' expresses the claim that George is Edward, which is false in every possible world. So, not knowing what context they are in, Alex can see that Edward is expressing either a necessary truth or a necessary falsehood. Neither of those would be useful information for her. But because she doesn't know what context they are in, and because Edward's claim is context sensitive, different rows determine different sets of worlds, so she cannot use the rows to decide what worlds to eliminate as possibilities.

Instead, she looks to the diagonal. If the world is an E world, then Edward has said something that is true in the context of utterance. But if the world is an F or a G world, then Edward has said something that is false in the context of utterance. So Alex has reason to eliminate the F and G worlds as possibilities, and she thus comes to know that she is in the E world, and hence that Edward is the speaker. Stalnaker's tools thus lets us give a better story about the informativeness of context-sensitive identity claims than is available in Kaplan's framework.

8.5 Stalnaker and Dynamic Pragmatics

Recall our earlier distinction between a *semantic* theory, which tells us what words and sentences mean, and a *pragmatic* theory, which tells us what speakers do with those meanings. Stalnaker presents his contextual subjectivism as involving both a semantic part and a pragmatic part. The semantic part is given by the two-dimensional charts. The theory of meaning assigns to each sentence a truth value relative to a pair of worlds. So in the semantic theory, Stalnaker like Lewis endorses double indexing. But Stalnaker then combines the double-indexed semantic theory with a pragmatic theory explaining how conversational participants adjust the state of conversational knowledge. Conversational knowledge is tracked using a set of worlds—the set of all worlds that, given what the conversational participants collectively know, might be actual. So to *update* the state of knowledge, we need to associate each utterance with a set of worlds. To do so, we use:

1. Rows, when all the rows of the two-dimensional chart are the same.
2. The diagonal, when the rows are different.

So at the level of the pragmatics, Stalnaker's theory doesn't use double-indexed truth conditions. Instead, it becomes a simple truth-conditional theory of the sort we set out in Chapter 4.

Stalnaker's approach can be thought of as a kind of *dynamic pragmatics*, because the pragmatic aspect of language that he is centrally interested in rules on how the use of language *changes* the conversational status. Subsequent work by Heim, Kamp, Veltman, and others has taken many of the same ideas but used them to set out a *dynamic semantics*, in which the core notion of the meaning of a sentence is *rules for changing the conversational status*. The dispute between dynamic-pragmatic and dynamic-semantic approaches is an ongoing one, with much of the discussion focusing on the comparative abilities of the two approaches to handle logically complex constructions involving conditionals and modals.

8.6 Final Thoughts on Formal Theorizing

The last two chapters have been difficult going. These two chapters give a taste of the sophisticated formal tools and associated conceptual disputes that theorizing about context sensitivity have produced. We have seen that Indexed Truth accounts can marshal a number of interesting devices for defending their theories against the Problems of Rigidity and Same-Saying. By combining double indexing with either same-saying skepticism or contextual subjectivism plus dynamic pragmatics, a theory can be produced that is a plausible rival for the Kaplan two-stage character-and-content theory.

Along the way, a number of important and difficult questions about background philosophical commitments are raised. Is truth a feature that sentences have relative to a world, or relative to a time, or relative to a more complex context that determines both a world and a time? Or is truth a feature that sentences have *absolutely*, rather than relative to anything at all? How do truth conditions and communicative effects of sentences relate to one another? How do context-sensitive expressions interact with other parts of the language, especially parts of the language that shift our attention to other worlds and times? Do context-sensitive expressions play an important role in allowing us to refer rigidly to objects without having a descriptive identification of those objects? How does what context-sensitive expressions *mean* interact with what we, as speakers, *do* with those expressions? None of these questions can be addressed at a satisfactory level of sophistication without first developing the sorts of formal tools we have explored in this section.

Not surprisingly, a central feature of all of the theoretical options we have considered is that sentences are evaluated relative to a *context*. But so far we have left the notion of a context rather unexamined. It has been important that contexts *determine* a time, or a location, or a speaker. But we have said nothing yet about what contexts are. In the final section of this book, we turn to this question, and some important philosophical consequences of how we answer it.

> CENTRAL POINTS IN CHAPTER 8

- Because an Indexed Truth theory does not separate out levels of character and content, it faces a challenge in accounting for patterns of agreement and disagreement among speakers using context-sensitive language.
- When combined with double indexing, Indexed Truth accounts allow us to define multiple ways of grouping sentences in contexts as saying the same thing.
- Lewis argues for propositional skepticism, denying that any one of these ways of grouping explains all of our ordinary practice of attributing agreement and disagreement.
- Stalnaker proposes a contextual subjectivism, on which we consider truth values relative to every context that by the conversational participants' lights might be the actual context.
- In simple cases with no relevant contextual ignorance, simple possible worlds contents can then be extracted.
- In more complicated cases with contextual ignorance, Stalnaker proposes a pragmatic mechanism of diagonalization, which lets him give a better account of the informativeness of certain sentences than Kaplan does.

QUESTIONS FOR CHAPTER 8

Comprehension Questions

8.1. Draw a table similar to the one on p. 143 for the sentences 'Today is Monday' and 'Yesterday was Monday', where contexts are specified by days, and worlds are either worlds in which it's Monday or worlds in which it's Tuesday (forget about the fact that in real life, it can be Monday in America and Tuesday in Britain).

8.2. Using a chart of the sort on p. 143, show how the Indexed Truth conditions of 'The president is a Democrat' and 'The actual president is a Democrat' differ. Then find a way of defining coarse-grained truth conditions along the lines of the worldly truth conditions defined above, so that the two sentences have the same coarse-grained truth conditions.

8.3. Now consider two people, one of whom says 'The president is a Democrat' and one of whom says 'The actual president is a Democrat'. Describe two scenarios, in one of which it would be natural to say that these two people agree and in one of which it would not be natural to say that they agree.

8.4. Consider the discussion on p. 144. Give two other worlds, in addition to WDO, that should remain live options, and two that shouldn't. Justify your choices.

8.5. Suppose Alex and Beth don't have any contextual ignorance, but are ignorant about whether Alex is happy. Give a Stalnaker-style model of this situation, and consider the two-dimensional charts for Alex's utterance of 'I am happy' and Beth's utterance of 'You are happy'. Explain why these charts give a good explanation of the sense in which Alex and Beth say the same thing.

Exploratory Questions

8.6. Suppose Alex, in addition to being uncertain where Alex is, is also uncertain where Beth is. So for all she knows, Alex might be in St Andrews and might be in Oslo, and Beth might be in St Andrews and might be in Oslo. And suppose also that Alex, struck with amnesia, no longer remembers who she is. So she does not know whether she is Alex or Beth.

Give a Stalnaker-style model of this situation. Specify sixteen worlds that are relevant to modeling the information in Alex's situation, and consider the two-dimensional chart giving the truth value of 'It is raining here' for pairs of those worlds. How should that set of worlds be updated by Alex's utterance? Does updating with the diagonal produce a plausible result?

8.7. Can Stalnaker's treatment of informative identity claims like 'I am Edward' be extended to informative identity claims like 'Superman is Clark Kent', which do not appear to involve any context-sensitive expressions?

> FURTHER READING FOR CHAPTER 8

For more on same-saying skepticism, see Cappelen and Lepore (2005).

For Stalnaker see his (1978) and his recent (2014) book. See Hawthorne and Magidor (2009) and Soames (2006) for challenges to Stalnaker's framework.

PART III

Contexts: What They Are and How We Create Them

This third part of the book addresses one overarching question: what is a context? We start by distinguishing two questions:

- What is it to be in a context?
- How does context determine the meaning of words?

We then consider two views of contexts—*The Low-Structure View* and *The High-Structure View*—to see how they can respond to these questions. We next turn to a more detailed discussion of what 'ingredients' a context must provide to account for gradable adjectives like 'rich', the second-person pronoun 'you', and other expressions and phenomena. We conclude this part of the book with a discussion of how speech itself can create contexts, what contextual accommodation and negotiation amounts to, and how asymmetric power relations affect such negotiations.

9
What are Contexts?

9.1 Where We Are and the Plan for This Chapter

In this book we have talked a lot about expressions that are context sensitive, and about theories of context sensitivity. An underlying issue we have not yet addressed directly is the question of what contexts *are*. In this part of the book, we turn to that and related questions.

We want to know what kinds of things contexts are so that we will know how to provide answers to two questions:

The Determination Question: Context-sensitive expressions have meanings relative to contexts. So whatever contexts are, they need to determine the meanings of these expressions. We need to be able to say what, for example, 'might' or 'fast' mean relative to a given context, so we need an account of contexts that lets us form the link between the context and the meanings of the context-sensitive vocabulary relative to that context.

The Possession Question: Speakers speak from contexts. When a particular speaker at a particular time says 'I am happy' or 'Alex is ready', they say something whose meaning depends on the context that is *their* context. So we need to be able to say which context is the speaker's context.

An adequate theory of what contexts are will help us answer both these questions. In this and the next chapter we primarily pursue a bottom-up approach: we look at a range of context-sensitive expressions to see what they tell us about the nature of contexts. In this chapter we investigate demonstratives (e.g. 'that') and how to understand so-called 'improper contexts' (e.g. cases where the person uttering (or writing) 'I' isn't the speaker). In the next chapter (Chapter 10) we then look at gradable adjectives, 'might', 'you', and presuppositions. Each of these has triggered extensive literatures over the last thirty years and understanding how they work will help illuminate what sort of things contexts are.

As we go through these cases it will prove useful to have two big picture theories of context in the background. We call them High-Structure and Low-Structure theories of contexts. To illustrate what we have in mind, consider some very simple ('toy') versions of these views—versions suited for dealing with (apparently) simple context-sensitive language like 'I', 'here', and 'now'. Here are the two options:

> **High-Structure Contexts (HS):** On this view, a context is an abstract object—more precisely it is a triple of a speaker, a location, and a time. So contexts are things like <Alex, St Andrews, June 1>, or <Beth, Oslo, July 7>.
>
> **Low-Structure Contexts (LS):** On this view, a context is a real-world event, e.g. the physical utterance. So contexts are things like Alex's saying 'I am happy' or Beth's saying 'Alex is here'.

We call the latter 'low structure' because it treats a context as a kind of lump: the context is just the whole big event e.g. of Alex speaking. So construed the context contains an enormous amount of 'things': e.g. Alex's socks, the chair she's sitting on, all the air molecules in the room, etc. The context, construed as the event itself, doesn't tell you (or highlight) which of these are semantically relevant—it doesn't semantically structure the event for you. The HS theory, on the other hand, does that work for you: it presents the semantically relevant components in a neat little pre-structured package for you.

As a result, HS theories are easier to use when constructing a theory of meaning. Most theories of meaning today operate with the HS notion of a context. However, one upshot of this chapter will be that neither theory does a better job at answering the two questions we started out with, i.e. the Possession and Determination questions. At the end of this chapter we tentatively conclude that *whatever problems the Low-Structure theory has in answering the Determination question, the High-Structure Theory has in answering the Possession question, and vice versa*. So insofar as our goal is to a get a theory of contexts that answers both questions, then either one would do.

To illustrate this point, we initially present demonstratives (i.e. 'that') and improper contexts as challenges to the LS view. However, as we will see, in neither case do we have a reason to prefer the LS theory over the HS theory. We simply move the problems from the Determination question to the Possession question.

So think of this chapter as having two goals: a) to introduce you to some interesting facts and theories about the expression 'that' and so-called 'improper contexts', and b) to show you that we have no good reason to prefer the HS theories to the LS theories.

9.2 Demonstratives and Context

Expressions like 'that' and 'those' are often called demonstratives. These are among the most useful tools of a language. For example, they enable us to talk about things we don't already have a word for. Alex, looking at a strange-looking animal—say a naked mole rat—can say: 'What is that?' He has managed to talk about the naked mole rat even though he has no word for it. More generally, we can use demonstratives to draw our audience's attention to things in our environment. For these and other reasons, it is a fundamental element of any natural language. Nonetheless, just how demonstratives work is a bit of a mystery. To see why this is a complex issue, ask yourself how the LS view can accommodate demonstratives. If the context just is the utterance (as the LS theorist holds), then we need to 'read off' from the utterance what the word 'that' refers to in that situation. How can this be done? Here are some options.

The (demonstrative) referent of an utterance of 'that' is:

- D1: The thing that the person who produced 'that' is pointing at.
- D2: The thing that the person who produced 'that' intends to talk about.
- D3: The most prominent object in the immediate environment of 'that'.

(For simplicity, we assume that our context has only one demonstrative referent. Sentences that use, for example, both 'this' and 'that' will need more than one demonstrative referent provided by their context. This will only add to the difficulties we're about to consider.)

On Pointing (D1): Suppose a proponent of the LS theory endorses D1, i.e. the rule that says the referent is picked out by a pointing. This rule is problematic for a number of reasons. First note that speakers can use the word 'that' without pointing to anything.

Extremely Salient Objects: Suppose Alex and Beth are talking, and a naked man goes running past them. Alex says to Beth, 'Wow, that was the president of the university'. Alex's use of the demonstrative 'that' refers to the naked man even without her pointing at him.

And speakers can point at objects without clearly referring to them with 'that'.

Mislocated Objects: Alex has a picture of Rudolf Carnap hanging on the wall behind her desk. Speaking to a student, she points behind her and says, 'That is a picture of the greatest philosopher of the twentieth century'. However, unbeknownst to her, the cleaning crew last night moved the picture to clean the wall, so it is now hanging five feet to the right of its usual location, and the part of the wall that Alex points to is empty. (Or perhaps Alex's hand is unsteady due to too many espressos that morning, and her shaking finger doesn't manage to target the picture.) Nevertheless, Alex's use of 'that' still plausibly refers to the picture.

And speakers can refer to one object by pointing at another.

Deferred Reference: Alex now unambiguously points to a picture of Carnap, but says instead 'That is the greatest philosopher of the twentieth century'. Her utterance does not say that the *picture* is the greatest philosopher, but rather that Carnap, the *subject* of the picture, is. Alex could similarly point to Carnap's name written down, or to Carnap's book *Meaning and Necessity*, and thereby secure reference to Carnap. (Perhaps pointing at a picture of Carnap just is a way to point at Carnap? Perhaps so, but then the notion of 'pointing' used in the clause for 'that' is more complicated than we might have expected. See the discussion of the 'demonstrated object' clause below. And in any case, pointing at the picture is also a way to point at the picture—see the discussion of **Too Many Referents** below.)

And it is not clear that 'what the speaker is pointing at' picks out any one thing even in the best of cases.

Too Many Referents: Human fingers are slightly bent, so there won't be any one line of pointing that the finger determines. And even when we can identify a reasonable line of pointing, there will typically be many possible targets. Alex points out the window and says, 'That is the Isle of May'. Is she pointing at the island? At a specific rock on the island? At a bird flying between her and the island? At the window? At air molecules between her and the window? At a region of space? Other factors (such as what Alex goes on to say after 'that') might lead us to prefer one of these choices over another, but the simple notion of pointing doesn't seem to provide a preferred candidate.

On Intentions (D2): Once we see the problems with the notion of pointing, it can be tempting for a proponent of LS theories of context to move to some version of D2: the referent of a demonstrative is whatever the speaker intends to refer to, and the pointing is just an external *clue* to the speaker's intentions. That's why Alex can, in a sense, point to Carnap by pointing to a picture of Carnap. The useful notion here is what Alex intends to refer to, and we identify the target of Alex's pointing in terms of her intentions.

However, this version of LS is also problematic: speakers can intend to refer to things that have nothing to do with the scene in front of speaker and audience, and in such cases, it's hard to accept that what the speaker intends to refer to is enough to determine a referent in context. Consider the following example due to Jeff King (2014: 5):

The Beach: Suppose I am sitting on Venice beach on a crowded holiday looking south. Hundreds if not thousands of people are in sight. I fix my attention on a woman in the distance and, intending to talk about her and gesturing vaguely to the south, say 'She is athletic'. You, of course, have no idea who I am talking about. It seems quite implausible in such a case to say that I succeed in securing the woman in question as the value of my demonstrative simply because I was perceiving her, and intending to talk about her.

King here even grants that the intention theory is further constrained by a requirement of perceptual contact. If we drop that constraint, then King's speaker could intend to refer to Mary Queen of Scots by 'she'. It would then be even more implausible that reference is secured, given the impossibility of an audience discovering this intention.

Kaplan (1970: 239), in a famous example, argues that when intentions and pointings come into conflict, pointings win out:

> **Agnew and Carnap:** Suppose that without turning and looking I point to the place on my wall which has long been occupied by a picture of Rudolf Carnap and I say: That is a picture of one of the greatest philosophers of the twentieth century. But unbeknownst to me, someone has replaced my picture of Carnap with one of Spiro Agnew.... I have said of a picture of Spiro Agnew that it pictures one of the greatest philosophers of the twentieth century. And my speech and demonstration suggest no other natural interpretation.... No matter how hard I intend Carnap's picture, I do not think it reasonable to call the content of my utterance true.

On Salience (D3): Finally, a proponent of LS might try to sweep both the pointing theory and the intention theory into a *salience* theory. On this approach, a demonstrative refers, on a given use, to whatever object is most salient for speaker and audience at the time of uttering—whatever object is most prominent in the environment, stands out the most, best grabs the attention of speaker and audience, and so on. We could then say that pointing at an object is one way to make it salient, and that speaker intentions will be recognizable, and hence effective in determining reference, when they target a salient object.

But without a theory of salience, it's hard to know what the real content is of the proposal that the referent is the most salient object in the immediate environment. Consider:

> **Extremely Salient Objects:** As the naked university presidence runs past, Alex points to a small bug on the grass and says, 'That is a ladybug'. Does her pointing really make the ladybug more salient than the naked president?

It's hard to believe that there is an independent notion of salience (that isn't just a theoretical name for *whatever demonstratives end up referring to*) that's being used here.

Furthermore in some cases demonstratives target objects that are in the immediate environment, let alone prominent, only in the most strained sense.

Future Demonstratives: Alex and Beth are watching *The Avengers*. As Loki steps out into Stuttgart Square, Alex whispers to Beth, 'This next scene is my favorite'. Alex's demonstrative refers to a scene that hasn't occurred yet, and that can't plausibly be considered salient.

Abstract Demonstratives: Alex and Beth are working on a complicated geometry problem. After staring at the diagram for a long time, Alex shouts 'That's the solution', and steps forward to draw a new line on the diagram. Alex's demonstrative refers to an abstract entity—a *way of solving the problem*, which can't plausibly be considered salient, and which Alex is taking a first step toward making clear by adding the line to the diagram.

Maybe all of these clauses were a mistake: the proponent of LS theories should only have said that the referent of an utterance of 'that' is *the object demonstrated in the utterance*. Pointings, intentions, and prominence could then all be part of a complicated package of factors that make an object the demonstrated object, but none of these would be the whole story. This is fine as far as it goes, but the worry is that it does not go very far. Absent an actual story about what it is for an object to be a demonstrated object, it seems to be equivalent to the claim that the referent of an utterance of 'that' is *the object that 'that' refers to, as used in the utterance* which is true, but uninformative.

The upshot is that answering the Determination question is quite challenging for the LS approach once we start considering demonstratives. But that doesn't mean we have a clear reason to prefer HS views. The HS view could make answering the Determination question easy: we could just expand the sequence (that is the context) with a slot for the demonstrated object. So far this is simple. However, none of the issues above are avoided; they just reoccur when trying to answer the Possession question. Answering the Possession question for the HS theorist is hard in exactly the same way that the Determination question became hard for the LS view. Recall, for example, the case of Extremely Salient Objects. The HS view has no difficulty with saying that the referent of 'that' relative to <Alex, L, T, naked president> is the naked president. But it *does* have difficulty in saying *why* Alex's context is the context <Alex, L, T, naked president>.

Taking stock: we've just seen two things. First, getting both the Determination question and the Possession question answered gets harder for *any* theory of context when we consider demonstratives. Second, those extra difficulties don't seem to give us any way of selecting between HS and LS approaches. All that the HS vs LS choice does is settle whether it's going to be the Determination question or the Possession question that gives us trouble, but we are in either case dealing with the same trouble, just distributed differently.

9.3 Improper Contexts

Over the last thirty years, there has been a great deal of interest in so-called *improper contexts*. These are contexts where, for example, the speaker of the context is not at the location of the context at the time of the context. The kinds of cases we have in mind are illustrated by messages left on answering machines. Consider Naomi who records on her home answering machine in Oslo a message 'I'm not here right now' on Tuesday. The recording is played back on Wednesday when Jill calls Naomi, at which time Naomi is visiting St Andrews. The message should communicate that Naomi is not in Oslo on Wednesday. 'Here' should pick out Oslo, and 'now' should pick out Wednesday. But neither Naomi's original utterance when recording the message nor the utterance by the answering machine when playing back the message has the right features:

- Naomi's original utterance is on Tuesday, and Naomi is in Oslo on Tuesday. This gets the place right, but the time wrong.
- The utterance by the answering machine is on Wednesday, and Naomi is in St Andrews on Wednesday. This gets the time right, but the place wrong.

What we want is the *time* of the answering machine speaking (Wednesday), but the *location* of Naomi originally speaking (Oslo).

The HS approach will thus tell us that we need the context <Naomi, Oslo, Wednesday>. This is an *improper* context, because Naomi is not in Oslo on Wednesday. That then looks like a problem for the LS approach. What 'low-structure' context can be provided? We might initially think that the LS approach just can't provide a context, because there is no utterance that is produced by Naomi on Wednesday in Oslo. But that's too quick. LS theorists can take answering machine cases to show that we need a more complicated answer to the Determination question. We don't, on this approach, need improper contexts. (Indeed, there *are* no improper contexts thought of in this way.) Rather, we need a rule that lets us extract improperly related referents for 'I', 'here', and 'now' from a particular utterance.

So how will the LS approach answer the Determination question? In the simplest answering machine cases, there are two events that are plausible candidates for the utterance—one is the event of Naomi's speaking into the answering machine, and the other is the event of Jill's hearing Naomi's message. We might have to stretch the notion of a 'producer' a bit to having Naomi come out as the producer of the second event, but it's not implausible that we can make things work out right. But it's not hard to find variants of the answering machine cases that are much harder for the LS account to analyze with clever choices of utterance. Consider:

> **Answering Service:** Naomi is moving to a new house in Chicago. She hasn't herself taken up residence in the house, but she has had phone service activated, and has had her belongings shipped to the new house. Before arriving there herself, she is vacationing in Rome. Realizing that she forgot to leave a message for her new home phone, on Tuesday she calls her answering service, which is housed in Seattle. Navigating an automatic system, she records a message saying 'I'm not here right now'. On Wednesday Jill calls Naomi's new number. No physical phone has been installed in Naomi's Chicago house. But after a few rings, a computer housed in the answering service's branch office in San Diego intercepts the call. Using a copy of the digital file of Naomi's recording sent from the Seattle office, it plays Naomi's message, which is heard by Jill in Miami from where she is calling.

We need an utterance that is produced by Naomi, is located in Chicago, and occurs on Wednesday, to get the right truth conditions. That's not Naomi's act of speaking, which was on Tuesday in Rome. And it's not the sound waves reaching Naomi, which are in Miami. And it's not the playback of Naomi's recording, which is in San Diego. No single thing seems to provide all the right pieces.

These cases look like they provide an advantage for the HS theories. However, as in the previous section, we'll now show that whatever complications the LS theories face are inherited by the HS theories. The reason is simple. While the HS theories have a simple account of what contexts are, they do not have a simple answer to the Possession question. Above we just assumed that a particular context (Naomi, Oslo, Wednesday) was the correct context for the interpretation of the message as replayed on Wednesday. But we haven't even started to answer the question: what *makes that the right context*? The answer, presumably, is some very complex story about the connection between Naomi's original speech (on Tuesday), her intentions, the interpreter's expectations, etc. Call this complex story 'Story'. Now, with Story in hand, we can use it to help out the LS theories. A proponent of an LS theory of contexts can say that the referent of an utterance of 'now' is whatever Story determines. Assuming Story is a good story for the HS theorist, it will do the work for the LS theorist as well. Any HS answer to the Possession question can be transformed into an LS answer to the Determination question.

CENTRAL POINTS IN CHAPTER 9

- We can distinguish two important questions about contexts: the Determination question and the Possession question.
- We can distinguish two kinds of theories of contexts: High-Structure Theories and Low-Structure Theories.
- Answering the Determination question is quite challenging for the LS approach once we start considering demonstratives, but that doesn't mean that we have clear reason to prefer HS views because answering the Possession question is hard for the HS view in exactly the same way that the Determination question became hard for the LS view.
- Improper contexts initially look like an advantage for the HS theories. That, however, turns out to be an illusion: HS theories have a simple account of what contexts are, but they do not have a simple answer to the Possession question.
- All that the HS vs LS choice does is settle whether it's going to be the Determination question or the Possession question that gives us trouble, but we are in either case dealing with the same trouble, just distributed differently.

WHAT ARE CONTEXTS? 163

QUESTIONS FOR CHAPTER 9

Comprehension Questions

9.1. Explore differences between one's natural judgments in the Spiro Agnew case and Alex's pointing at the picture case.
9.2. Consider answers to our questions for the LS and HS views of context for some other context-sensitive expression of your choosing.
9.3. Explain in your own words the difference between low and high-structure views of contexts.
9.4. The text suggested there wasn't much to decide between the two views: explain why, and whether you agree.

Exploratory Questions

9.5. Maybe the Determination question isn't really so easy for the LS views to answer. Consider two kinds of worries:
- Utterances take time, so 'the time of the utterance' doesn't tell us exactly what time to use in interpreting 'now' in context.
- An utterance is in many places simultaneously. Alex's utterance is in St Andrews, and in Scotland, and in Europe, and in the Edgecliffe building, and in room G03. So 'the location of the utterance' doesn't tell us which of these places to use in interpreting 'here' in context.

How should we respond to these worries? Try to construct cases with 'now' and 'here' that are sensitive to these sorts of variations, and see if judgments about such cases provide any helpful data for thinking about the worries.

9.6. Can answering machine cases be analyzed using the resources of double indexing? Consider whether the need for improper contexts can be avoided using only proper contexts, but then shifting the values of some contextual parameters in the 'shiftable' position of a double-indexed account to capture the answering machine data.

FURTHER READING FOR CHAPTER 9

For various answers to the question of what contexts are, see Gauker (1998), Lewis (1979), chapter 1 of Stalnaker (2014), Bianchi (2003), and the papers in Finkbeiner, Meibauer, and Schumacher (2012).

Problems like the Spiro Agnew case have been extensively discussed: see, for example, Gauker (2008) and Stokke (2010). Answering machine cases go back to Predelli (1998); for a nice overview see Cohen and Michaelson (2013).

For a general discussion of the demands demonstratives place on a theory of context, see Caplan (2003).

10
More on Contextual Ingredients

10.1 Where We Are and the Plan for This Chapter

The previous chapter concluded that it made no significant difference whether we operate with a Low-Structure (LS) or High-Structure (HS) view of contexts. In this chapter we will use a framework that operates with a HS conception of context. We then ask: what ingredients are needed as parts of those structures? Much of the work on context sensitivity over the last forty years has focused on how to understand the specific features of contexts that specific linguistic constructions are sensitive to. In this chapter we outline some issues that come up in connection with four kinds of expressions:

- Gradable Adjectives.
- Epistemic 'Mights'.
- The second-person pronoun, 'you'.
- Presuppositions.

The overall goal is to reemphasize a point we made at the end of Chapter 7: as in the case of a theory of meaning, our understanding of what contexts are is often driven by very detailed investigations into the use and meaning of particular expressions. So in the current literature, one will find a very great deal of investigation into specific expressions and the demands these put on our overall theory. The methodology is thus bottom up: start with specific expressions and then work our way up to an overall theory of contexts.

10.2 Gradable Adjectives

In the first and third chapters we observed that *gradable adjectives* create context sensitivity. The sentence 'Naomi is rich' can be true when uttered by impoverished graduate students, but false when uttered by investment bankers (even if Naomi's net worth doesn't change). What ingredient in context then controls the interpretation of gradable adjectives?

One natural thought is that gradable adjectives require *comparison classes*. 'Naomi is rich' would thus mean something like *Naomi is rich for an X*, or *Naomi is richer than the average X*, where X specifies some class of people. Context would then be required to provide the value for X. If this is right, then contexts, in addition to tangible elements like speakers, times, and places, require more abstract ingredients like comparison classes. And contexts will need *a lot* of these comparison classes. Suppose we are in a context C in which saying 'Naomi is rich' means that Naomi is rich for an investment banker. Then C provides the comparison class *investment banker*. But it doesn't follow that:

- In C, 'Naomi is fast' means 'Naomi is fast for an investment banker'
- In C, 'Naomi is amusing' means 'Naomi is amusing for an investment banker'
- In C, 'Naomi is devout' means 'Naomi is devout for an investment banker'

Different gradable adjectives, even in the same context, can call for different comparison classes. So contexts need to come supplied with enough comparison classes to handle all of the gradable adjectives that might in that context be used. Answering the Possession question—saying what it is about the actual speech situation that determines these many comparison class ingredients of context—will be a difficult.

A full theory of the contextual contribution to gradable adjectives can't just provide comparison classes for all of the many gradable adjectives, though. We've just noted that many gradable adjectives are independent of one another—the comparison class for 'rich' needn't be the same as the comparison class for 'fast'. But not all gradable adjectives are independent. In a context in which 'Naomi is rich' means that Naomi is rich for an investment banker, the sentence 'Naomi is poor' will have to mean that Naomi is poor *for an investment banker*. These two adjectives get tied to the same comparison class. And 'Alex's car is expensive' will tend to mean *expensive for a car of an investment banker*. So a more adequate theory will need to link gradable adjectives into clusters that are tied to the same comparison class.

One way to take a step in this direction is to rethink the idea of comparison classes. Our starting idea was that the comparison class for 'rich' would be some bunch of people exhibiting richness to varying extents. But perhaps what we need instead is a *scale* of wealth, and then a contextually provided *point* on that scale. 'Naomi is rich' would then mean that Naomi's wealth, measured on that scale, was above the contextually specified point. Then the clustering of gradable adjectives could be handled by associating multiple gradable adjectives with the same scale. 'Rich' and 'poor' measure on one scale, and get their content relative to a contextually provided point on that scale. 'Tall' and 'short' measure on a second scale, and get their content relative to a different contextually provided point on that scale.

One piece of evidence in favor of this 'scales' view comes from the availability of gradable adjective comparisons. We can compare different objects with respect to a single gradable adjective:

1. The tree is as tall as the building is tall.

It's hard to know how to interpret (1) using comparison classes—are we using trees as the comparison class, or buildings, or something else? But using scales gives us a straightforward interpretation. There is a single scale of linear distance, and the tree and the building measure to the same point on that scale. A further consideration favoring scales over comparison classes is that comparing different objects with respect to different gradable adjectives is sometimes possible and sometimes not possible. A claim like:

2. Naomi is as tall as the desk is long

is fine, but:

3. The tree is as tall as Alex is clever

is bad.

With scales, we can explain acceptability of cross-adjectival comparisons by tying the comparable adjectives to the same scale, and the unacceptability of other comparisons by tying the incomparable adjectives to different scales. Again, if we rely on comparison classes, it is hard to see what explanation of the comparability and incomparability data is available.

If the scale approach is right, it yields a prediction: cross-adjectival comparability should be *transitive*. 'Tall' and 'long', as we've seen above, are cross-comparable. And 'long' and 'wide' are also cross-comparable:

4. The desk is as long as the bed is wide.

The 'scales' theory explains this by supposing that 'tall' and 'long' use the same scale, and that 'long' and 'wide' use the same scale. But then 'tall' and 'wide' need to use that scale, so 'tall'/ 'wide' comparisons should be possible:

5. Naomi is as tall as the bed is wide.

Is this prediction always born out? In the right contexts, we can cross-adjectivally compare 'sweet' and 'salty':

6. The caramel ice cream is sweeter than it is salty.

And in the right contexts, we can cross-adjectivally compare 'salty' and 'sweaty':

7. After a long run on a dry hot day, his shirt is saltier than it is sweaty.

But it doesn't obviously follow that we can cross-adjectivally compare 'sweet' and 'sweaty'.

Getting a full account of how scales might work, and hence on how scalar degree information might serve as an ingredient in context, is a difficult matter. Here are two examples of the sort of problems that current work on gradable adjectives continues to grapple with. A full theory of scales needs to explain why *sometimes* cross-scalar comparisons are acceptable:

8. The work is as hard as the day is long.

We also need to explain why 'negative' and 'positive' adjectives associated with the same scale can't be used in cross-adjectival comparisons:

BAD: Naomi is as rich as Jill is poor.
GOOD: Naomi is shorter than the ceiling is low.
BAD: Naomi is taller than the ceiling is low.

10.3 Epistemic 'Mights'

In Chapter 1 we used so-called epistemic 'mights' as an example of a context-sensitive expression. What aspect of context are they sensitive to? Let's consider first the Simple Story:

The Simple Story: What the speaker knows. According to this proposal John's utterance of 'The keys might be on the kitchen table' means that for all he, i.e. John, knows, the keys might be on the kitchen table. John speaks truly as long as what he knows doesn't rule out the keys being there.

This account explains why John can say something true by uttering that sentence, and Tim can simultaneously say something true by uttering: 'The keys can't be on the table'. If Tim has checked, and so knows that the keys are not on the table, then his utterance would be true. Their utterances are sensitive to different contextual features: Tim's assertion is sensitive to what Tim knows and John's assertion is sensitive to what John knows. On this epistemic modals pick up bodies of knowledge from the context—and, more specifically, they pick up the speaker's body of knowledge.

However, most theorists don't think the Simple Story can be right. Here are three examples that seem to undermine the Simple Story:

Example a: Suppose Tim observes John looking for the keys. Tim knows the keys are on the kitchen table, but he doesn't want to tell John where they are. John asks whether the keys are in the kitchen. Tim says, 'They might be. They might not be' (this is based on an example in Egan, Hawthorne, and Weatherson (2005: 140)).

According to Egan, Hawthorne, and Weatherson, Tim is obviously being unhelpful, but he is not lying. If what he says is true, then the Simple Story cannot be right (since he knows they are in the kitchen, so he shouldn't be able to truly say 'They might not be').

Example b: Ann is planning a surprise party for Bill. Unfortunately, Chris has discovered the surprise and told Bill all about it. Now Bill and Chris are having fun watching Ann try to set up the party without being discovered. Currently Ann is walking past Chris' apartment carrying a large supply of party hats. She sees a bus on which Bill frequently rides home, so she jumps into some nearby bushes to avoid being spotted. Bill, watching from Chris' window, is quite amused, but Chris is puzzled and asks Bill why Ann is hiding in the bushes. Bill says:

(2) I might be on that bus. (Egan, Hawthorne, and Weatherson (2005: 140))

It seems Bill has, somehow, conveyed the correct explanation for Ann's dive—he's said something that's both true and explanatory. The Simple Story cannot explain how Bill's utterance of (2) can be true. Bill knows that he is in Chris' apartment and so knows that he is not on that bus (so it is not compatible with what he knows that he is on the bus).

Example c: Go back to the original example involving John and Tim, where John says something true by uttering 'The keys might be on the kitchen table' and Tim says something true by uttering 'The keys might not be on the kitchen table'. Now, change the case a bit so that Tim hears what John is saying. He could respond by saying 'No, that's not right—I checked they are not there'. Note that if what John's original utterance meant was that it is compatible with John's body of knowledge that the keys are on the kitchen table (i.e. if what context contributes is the speaker's body of information), then Tim is wrong to say 'No, that's not right', because what John said is sensitive only to what John knows. What Tim knows makes no difference to the interpretation of what John said.

Taking stock: What these and related cases shows is that it is spectacularly difficult to figure out just what elements we need from context to interpret utterances of epistemic modals. The Simple Story is far too simple. There are now industrial-scale efforts being put into figuring out just what the right story is for epistemic modals. Whatever it ends up being, it will no doubt add exotic components to what we think of as contexts.

10.4 You: Audience Sensitivity?

In Chapter 1 we discussed a set of expressions that we collectively labeled the Basic Set: 'I', 'that', 'now', 'yesterday', etc. They initially seemed fairly straightforward, but we have gradually seen that veneer of simplicity fade away: it turns out both 'I' and 'that' are massively difficult to understand. We turn now to another expression that initially might appear simple: 'you'. Surely, one might think at first, 'you' simply denotes the addressee that the speaker has in mind. As in the other cases, this appearance of simplicity fades as soon as we start looking at a broader range of data. Here is an important example, discussed at length by Andy Egan (2009: 259).

(Billboard) Horton produces a billboard on which is written the sentence, 'Jesus loves you'. Call the context in which this occurs Inscribe. Frank and Daniel each drive past the billboard and read it.

Egan asks: 'What is the message that the billboard conveys to Frank? What does Frank need to come to accept to take on board what the billboard says?' The simple story about 'you' tells us that it refers to some person (or group) intended by the speaker. But how can Horton have had Frank in mind? He had no idea that Frank would drive past his billboard. As an effort to bolster the simple story about 'you', one could try out the suggestion that 'you' refers to, for example, the group of all those people who will ever read the billboard. Call this group G. So Horton's intention was for 'you' to refer to G, and even if he doesn't know exactly who the members of G are—i.e. he can't list them individually—we have no problem understanding how 'you' can denote a group even when the speaker doesn't know all the members of the group (a speaker in a room can say: 'Can you all pick up a handout?', referring to all the people in the room, even though she doesn't know who they all are). Egan, however, makes a good case that this isn't the right way to understand the interpretation of billboards: 'In general, we ought to say that the billboard expresses, to each reader, the relevant singular proposition about *them*. (To reinforce this intuition, think about the effect of follow-up billboards a bit further down the road that read 'I mean you!', or 'that's right, buddy—*you*!'.)' (Egan 2009: 259).

If we go along with Egan and say that there are two different contents expressed, one for Frank and one for Daniel, this has wide-reaching implications for our account of context sensitivity. If we have just one utterance, in one context, with one speaker, we can, within the frameworks we have worked with so far, get only one content. Utterance+ and Context gives us one content. What seems to be going on in the Billboard case is that we get one content for each interpreter. If this is right, then the interpreter might have to be included in the relevant contextual parameters. Furthermore, we might have to recognize that any utterance can have more than one interpreter and so can have different contents relative to different interpreters. Egan takes this to show that the principle he calls Speaker Only is false:

Speaker Only: Once we've fixed which sentence was uttered, content depends only on features of the speaker's...context. Context-sensitive vocabulary is only sensitive to features of the speaker's situation at the time of utterance.

Billboard and related cases are evidence of Audience Sensitivity:

Audience Sensitivity: For some uses of context-sensitive vocabulary, the contribution that they make to the content of sentences in which they occur is sensitive not (merely) to features of the speaker's predicament, but (also) to features of the predicaments of particular audience members.

10.5 Presupposition

One marker of context sensitivity that we have focused on is that a context-sensitive sentence can vary its truth value from context to context—in one context, 'I am happy' is true; in another context, 'I am happy' is false. But there is another kind of contextual variation in truth value that we can observe. Compare the following two discourses:

1. Alex is starting graduate school in philosophy next fall. Beth wants to be a philosopher, too.
2. Charles is starting graduate school in linguistics next fall. Beth wants to be a philosopher, too.

Assume that Beth does want to be a philosopher. Then the second sentence of the first discourse is straightforwardly true. But the same sentence occurring as the second sentence of the second discourse is not straightforwardly true. We wouldn't want to say that it's false, but neither would we want to say that it is true—it is rather in some way strange, inappropriate, and perhaps unevaluable. So in one context, 'Beth wants to be a philosopher too' is true, but in another context 'Beth wants to be a philosopher too' is neither true nor false. Its truth value contextually varies from true to neither true nor false.

Similar cases show contextual variation in what follows from a sentence. Compare the following three sentences:

1. Beth doesn't realize her car has been stolen.
2. If Beth hasn't looked out the window yet, she doesn't realize her car has been stolen.
3. If Beth's car has been stolen, she doesn't realize her car has been stolen.

The first of these sentences implies that Beth's car has been stolen. That implication survives when it is put in the context of the first conditional, but disappears when it is put in the context of the second conditional.

Both of these examples feature the phenomenon of *presupposition*. Some sentences presuppose that the audience is already aware of certain information. Consider the sentence 'Alex regrets stealing Beth's car'. This sentence directly reports an attitude of Alex's, but it presupposes as background information that Alex did in fact steal Beth's car. If we negate this sentence and form 'Alex doesn't regret stealing Beth's car', the presupposition remains—the negated sentence continues to presuppose that Alex stole Beth's car, but now reports that Alex doesn't feel regret about having done so.

In a given context, the presuppositions of a sentence might or might not be met. In one context, we are all aware that Alex stole Beth's car. In this context, an utterance of 'Alex regrets stealing Beth's car' will be incorporated smoothly, perhaps resolving some uncertainty some of us have about how Alex feels about her criminal deed. In another context, only the speaker realizes that Alex stole Beth's car. In this context, an utterance of 'Alex regrets stealing Beth's car' will be received quite differently. Since the audience did not share the presupposition, the utterance will be met with resistance and surprise. 'Hey, wait a minute—I didn't realize that Alex had stolen Beth's car!' is a plausible response.

Utterances of presuppositional sentences thus vary contextually depending on whether the audience accepts what is presupposed. When the presupposition is accepted, the sentence is viewed as true or false as normal. But when the presupposition is not accepted, the sentence is viewed as anomalous or defective, rather than true or false. An adequate theory of context needs to provide some ingredient that determines how presuppositional sentences are interpreted.

What is needed is a *body of information*. A presuppositional sentence S presupposes some claim P. (For example, 'Beth wants to be a philosopher, too' presupposes something like 'Someone other than Beth wants to be a philosopher'.) The context has as an ingredient some body of information. If P is implied by that information, S is acceptable in context; if P isn't implied by that information, S is received as defective.

Answering the Possession question for presuppositional contexts—that is, determining *what* body of information goes into context in a specific speech situation—is a complicated matter. Information that is taken by all of the conversational participants to be background common knowledge tends to be in the body of information. This is why it is normally acceptable to say:

- My car's steering wheel is black.

but not:

- My car's giraffe is tall.

For any X, 'My car's X' presupposes that my car has an X. It is background common knowledge that cars normally have steering wheels, but not usually background common knowledge that cars have giraffes. In the right conversation, though, it might be (imagine a car dealership that puts free stuffed giraffes in their cars; if one car buyer says to another: 'My car's giraffe is tall', that's fine). Explicit utterances earlier in the conversation can also help shape the body of information. The difference between the two discourses about Beth wanting to be a philosopher with which we started this discussion is that in one, the presupposing sentence was preceded by an explicit utterance whose informational content satisfied the presupposition of 'too', but in the other, it was not.

Examples like 'If Beth's car has been stolen, she doesn't realize it has been' reveal a further complication in the informational structure of context. 'Beth realizes that her car has been stolen' presupposes that Beth's car has been stolen, and so should be acceptable only in a context that includes the information that Beth's car has been stolen. The conditional 'If Beth's car has been stolen, she doesn't realize it has been stolen' doesn't put that information into context in the same way that 'Alex is starting graduate school in philosophy next fall. Beth wants to be a philosopher, too.' puts its presupposed information into context. After the conditional has been uttered, it remains an open question whether Beth's car has been stolen. But what the conditional does do is create a smaller 'local context' used just for evaluating the consequent of the conditional, and add to the local context the information that Beth's car has been stolen. Examples like this show that we may need more than one context at a time, and possibly elaborate hierarchical relations among contexts.

Sometimes when a sentence is uttered with an unsatisfied presupposition, we use it to *change* the context, adding what was presupposed to the contextual body of information. When a store posts a sign saying 'We regret that we cannot accept personal checks', they use the presuppositional word 'regret'. The sign thus presupposes that the store cannot accept personal checks. But it wasn't already common background knowledge that the store didn't accept checks—rather, the store owners are leveraging the phenomenon of presupposition to use this sign to *enter into* the contextual information the no-checks policy. This process of changing the contextual information with presuppositions is called *accommodation*. Accommodation is the beginning of a large subject of studying the *two-way* structure of context sensitivity, in which not only does context shape linguistic interpretation, but also linguistic interpretation shapes context.

CENTRAL POINTS IN CHAPTER 10

- Our understanding of what contexts are is often driven by very detailed investigations into the use and meaning of particular expressions. Contexts are whatever can help us explain the behavior of context-sensitive expressions.
- Gradable adjectives require scales, comparison classes, and ways of connecting these.
- Epistemic modals require that we be able to specify the relevant body of knowledge. It has proven very hard to specify what the relevant body of knowledge is.
- The second-person pronoun, 'you', behaves in ways that seem to be sensitive to the audience's context, not just the speaker. If this is correct, then we need two sets of contexts: Speaker's context and audience's context.
- Presuppositions require that context provide a 'body of information'. This is information that is sometimes assumed to be shared by conversational participants, sometimes not.
- Presuppositions within conditionals also require that we distinguish between global and local contexts.

QUESTIONS FOR CHAPTER 10

Comprehension Questions

10.1. Can you think of other acceptable cross-scalar comparisons?

10.2. Suppose John says 'The keys might be on the table', and Tim then responds, 'No, that's not right. I checked and they aren't there'. It seems that John could respond to Tim's utterance in either of two ways:
- Oh, then I guess I was wrong.
- I didn't say they were on the table. I only said they might be on the table. And they might have been. So I was right.

How can we make sense of both of these responses being acceptable?

10.3. Give another case like Egan's billboard case. Explain how your case creates problems for standard theories of context possession.

10.4. Give three more examples of expressions that presuppose the audience is in possession of some body of information to be sensibly uttered. Explain what is presupposed by each.

Exploratory Questions

10.5. Egan claims that Horton's billboard conveys to Frank the singular proposition that Jesus loves Frank, and to Susan the singular proposition that Jesus loves Susan. This then creates different contents expressed by the billboard for Frank and for Susan, which is what causes the problem for standard theories of context dependency. But do we need to accept Egan's characterization of the case? Consider the alternative view that the billboard expresses the general proposition that Jesus loves everyone, or perhaps that Jesus loves everyone who sees it. Frank and Susan could then reach the particular conclusions that Jesus loves Frank and that Jesus loves Susan by a quick bit of logical reasoning from that general proposition. And we would have no need for separate contexts for separate interpreters.

Consider how some additional cases might bear on choosing between Egan's interpretation of the case and the 'general proposition' interpretation:

- A more exclusive church puts up a billboard reading 'Jesus loves you, and no one else'. (Is there something contradictory about the billboard?)
- The radio announcer says, 'Don't touch that dial! We'll be right back'. (Does this order require that no one touch any dial?)

Also, consider whether the same phenomenon can occur with other context-sensitive expressions. Suppose the billboard says 'Jesus wants you to be ready!'. Can this billboard convey to Frank that Jesus wants Frank to be ready for his exam, and to Susan that Jesus wants Susan to be ready to go swimming?

10.6. We can model bodies of information using sets of possible worlds. Let's start with the idea that a body of information is a set of context-insensitive sentences. Given any such sentence S, there is a set W(S) of all and only the possible worlds relative to which S is true. Then given a body of information B, given as a set of sentences, we can define the worldly body W(B) to be the intersection of all of the W(S), for S in B.

Show the following about worldly bodies:

If sentence P implies sentence Q, and B is a body of information containing P but not Q, and B' is the body of information that results from adding Q to B', then W(B) = W(B').

Is this a good feature or a bad feature? If it's a bad feature, it presumably gives us some reason to prefer sentential bodies of information to worldly bodies. What would go wrong if we used worldly bodies?

10.7. The previous exercise suggested that the body of information that presupposition needs as an ingredient of context might be modeled by a set of possible worlds. We've also seen that modals plausibly need a set of possible worlds to be an ingredient of context. This then suggests the simplifying thought that presuppositions and modals might both use the same ingredient. If that is right, it predicts certain consequences. Let S be a sentence that presupposes that P, for some P. Let W(P) be the set of worlds relative to which P is true. Explain why S will then be acceptable only in a context whose set-of-worlds ingredient is a subset of W(P).

Now consider the claim: It might be that not P. Explain why this sentence will not be acceptable in any context whose set-of-worlds ingredient is a subset of W(P).

FURTHER READING FOR CHAPTER 10

Further reading on gradable adjectives and 'might' can be found in Chapter 1.
For presupposition, see Beaver and Geurts (2011).
For more on audience sensitivity, see Cappelen (2008a) and (2008b), and Davis (2013).

11

How Speech Creates Contexts
Negotiation and Accommodation

11.1 Where We Are and the Plan for This Chapter

Contexts don't exist independently of the speech that takes place in them. That we speak is itself an important aspect of the contexts we are in when we speak. Right now, you, our reader, are probably sitting quietly reading. If you were to say something out loud, you have changed the context you are in. Suddenly you are in a context where speech takes place and you are the speaker. In various ways, speech itself is an important part of the context that shapes the meaning of words in that context. As a result, the context of speech, the speech itself, and the meaning of that speech are difficult to disentangle. They are interdependent in complicated ways. This final chapter explores some of those interconnections.

11.2 Lewis on Accommodation and Black Magic: How Speech Creates Context

In the paper 'Scorekeeping in a Language Game', David Lewis (1979: 346) contrasts conversations with games, such as baseball:

> Suppose the batter walks to first base after only three balls. His behavior would be correct play if there were four balls rather than three. That's just too bad—his behavior does not at all make it the case that there are four balls and his behavior is correct. Baseball has no rule of accommodation to the effect that if a fourth ball is required to make correct the play that occurs, then that very fact suffices to change the score so that straightway there are four balls.

Conversations are different. We change the context in such a way that what the speaker says comes out true. Here are three examples to illustrate the process Lewis has in mind. The first is from Richard Holton (2003: 290):

> When I say that we can't now get to London in time for the conference, I don't mean that it is physically impossible to do so: a speed far short of the speed of light would take us there with hours to spare. Nor need I even mean that a chartered private helicopter that took us door to door would be too slow. Rather I mean that none of the standard options, the kind of thing that we might be prepared to pay for, would get us there in time.

So when Holton uses 'can' in the original sentence, that has to be interpreted against assumptions about what are normal options—it is the claim that none of those options would get them to the conference in time. The central point is this: *'this context doesn't need to be already in place: uttering my sentence puts it in place, and so provides the context against which my utterance can be true'* (our emphasis, Holton (2003: 290)). The required contextual parameters (i.e. something like 'consider only standard travel options') were not in place before Holton spoke (for all we know the previous conversation might have been about spaceships); they became the relevant contextual parameters as a result of the speech itself. In some sense, the context relevant for interpreting the claim came into existence as a result of the speech itself.

The second example is from Lewis (1979: 348). He asks us to consider utterances of the following two sentences:

- The pig is grunting, but the pig with floppy ears is not grunting
- The dog got in a fight with another dog

The only way these could be true (and surely they could be) is for 'the pig' and 'the dog' to 'denote one of two pigs or dogs, both of which belong to the domain of discourse' (Lewis (1979)). This is work for a theory of contexts. How can a context provide what we need, i.e. separate pigs for each occurrence of 'pig' and separate dogs for each occurrence of 'dog'? Here is Lewis' (1979: 348) suggestion:

> The proper treatment of descriptions must be more like this: 'the F' denotes x if and only if x is the most salient F in the domain of discourse, according to some contextually determined salience ranking. The first of our two sentences means that the most salient pig is grunting but the most salient pig with floppy ears is not. The second means that the most salient dog got in a fight with some less salient dog.

According to this proposal, the reference of 'the F' is determined by salience—it picks out a salient F. But what makes something salient? One of the ways in which we can raise something to salience is *through talking about it*. In other words, what is salient in a context (and so determines the referent of what we talk about, e.g. the referent of 'the cat' or 'the pig') is determined by the conversation itself—talk and context are not independent entities. Here is Lewis (1979: 348-9) illustrating this point:

Imagine yourself with me as I write these words. In the room is a cat, Bruce, who has been making himself very salient by dashing madly about. He is the only cat in the room, or in sight, or in earshot. I start to speak to you:

> The cat is in the carton. The cat will never meet our other cat, because our other cat lives in New Zealand. Our New Zealand cat lives with the Cresswells. And there he'll stay, because Miriam would be sad if the cat went away.

At first, 'the cat' denotes Bruce, he being the most salient cat for reasons having nothing to do with the course of conversation. If I want to talk about Albert, our New Zealand cat, I have to say 'our other cat' or 'our New Zealand cat.' But as I talk more and more about Albert, and not any more about Bruce, I raise Albert's salience by conversational means. Finally, in the last sentence of my monologue, I am in a position to say 'the cat' and thereby denote not Bruce but rather the newly-most-salient cat Albert.

Notice the analogy with Holton's case: According to Holton, we accommodated his use of 'can't now get to London in time'—i.e. the conversational participants let the transportation options be the 'normal' ones, and we do that to make his utterance come out true. Something similar goes on with uses of 'the cat' in the example above. Albert ends up being the most salient cat because of the very speech in which 'the cat' refers to Albert (Lewis' speech has created the contextual conditions required for its own correct interpretation).

In light of such cases, Lewis (1979: 34) articulates what he calls 'the Rule of Accommodation':

Rule of Accommodation: If at time t something is said that requires, if it is to be acceptable, that x be more salient than y; and if, just before t1, x is no more salient than y; then—ceteris paribus and within certain limits—at t, x becomes more salient than y.

Angelika Kratzer (1981: 61) calls this *black magic*:

If the utterance of an expression requires a complement of a certain kind to be correct, and the context just before the utterance does not provide it, then ceteris paribus and within certain limits, a complement of the required kind comes into existence. This is black magic, but it works in many cases.

In the previous chapter, we saw an example of accommodation in the context of presupposition. Here we will consider one more illustration of accommodation at work.

Standards of precision vary between contexts. What is precise enough in one context isn't in another. J. L. Austin (1962: 143) provides the example:

- 'France is hexagonal'.

In some contexts, this is precise enough for conversational purposes, and so we treat it as true (or as Lewis says, 'true enough'). There are of course many contexts where it would be wildly inappropriate—those are contexts where the standards of precision are higher. According to Lewis (1979: 352), we again see the rule of accommodation at work:

> One way to change the standards is to say something that would be unacceptable if the standards remained unchanged. If you say 'Italy is boot-shaped' and get away with it, low standards are required and the standards fall if need be, thereafter 'France is hexagonal' is true enough. But if you deny that Italy is boot-shaped, pointing out the differences, what you have said requires high standards under which 'France is hexagonal' is far from true enough.

Again the central thought is this: *a feature of context that was not in place before the speech act happened is put in place because of that very speech act. The very context that determines the content of a speech act is, in part, created by (or shaped by) that very speech act.* The contrast with games is sharp: There the rules are in place and we don't accommodate to make moves successful. If you miss a basket in basketball, you've missed. We don't move the basket to accommodate your shot. If Lewis is right, speech is different: we constantly adjust contexts to accommodate speakers.

11.3 When We Don't Accommodate: Negotiation

Accommodation takes place when the conversation partners try to help each other out. But conversation partners are not always cooperative. Many conversational contexts are confrontational, or at least not fully cooperative. Here is an illustration inspired by an example from Mark Richard (2004: 218): imagine two speakers, Didi and Naomi, who disagree about whether to apply the word 'rich' to a friend, Mary. Mary, we can imagine, has just won a million-dollar lottery. For Didi, that's enough to classify Mary as 'rich'. Naomi, however, doesn't think a million dollars is all that much. She's unimpressed and refuses to apply 'rich' to Mary. So they seem to be in disagreement. In conversation, neither one is backing down. The disagreement persists. Note that this disagreement seems not to be due to any disagreement about the objective or non-linguistic facts. They agree about how much money Mary has and about her level of wealth relative to others. They are in disagreement about how the term 'rich' ought to be used. And this disagreement reflects a disagreement about what counts as a luxury, what counts as a necessity, and what counts as having *significantly* more than average wealth. In some sense they have a substantive disagreement about what it is to be rich, and that is reflected in their disagreement about how to use 'rich'. How, in such a context, will the meaning of 'rich' be fixed? In their joint context neither one wants to accommodate the other. What happens? We can describe the process as a form of negotiation over meaning or over context that determines meaning. But what is negotiation over meaning? How do we do it? Does it matter? We'll start with the last question and then move to the first two.

11.4 Why We Negotiate Over Meanings

11.4.1 *First motivation for meaning negotiation: to avoid verbal disputes*

At first glance, it might seem that we simply shouldn't care about meaning negotiation. If Didi uses the word 'rich' in one way and Naomi in another, let them just go ahead and use the term in their respective ways. Of course, it is bad if they are unaware of the difference in usage. Then they would be talking past each other. If they are unaware of their different usage, they would have what is call a 'verbal dispute' (see Chalmers 2011, Jenkins 2014). We try to coordinate on meanings in a context so that communication will go more smoothly. In particular, we want to avoid verbal disputes. If Didi utters 'Mary is rich' and Naomi utters 'No, Didi is not rich!', but unbeknownst to each other use the word 'rich' in different ways, then they are simply talking past each other. If one participant in the conversation refuses to accommodate, they should try to figure out how to resolve their disagreement. Otherwise this becomes a wasted communicative effort.

> **Observation #9.1** *Verbal Disputes and Meaning Negotiation in Philosophy*
>
> As we just said, verbal disputes arise when conversational participants use the same words with different meanings and are unaware of doing it. Some philosophers, prominently David Chalmers (2011) (see also Cohen forthcoming), think much of philosophy is plagued by pointless verbal disputes. Here is an alternative way to think. Much philosophical debate is in effect an exercise in meaning negotiation and these are not pointless. Terms like 'knowledge', 'justice', 'causation', 'belief', 'justification', 'virtue', 'color', 'science', 'action', and 'life' are all arguably terms that have many potential meanings. There are many admissible uses of those terms. Philosophers are not having substantive disputes over these topics; they are, instead, negotiating meanings. However, the argument goes, they are not aware of doing so. They think they are engaged in substantive disputes over knowledge, justice, virtue, and so on. Instead, they disagree over how words *should* be used, not over anything non-linguistic. (See Chalmers (2011), Ludlow (2014), Plunket and Sundell (2013), Cohen (forthcoming).) If these arguments are right, it is particularly important for philosophers to understand and be able to identify meaning negotiation and to know how to distinguish it from a verbal dispute.

11.4.2 Second motivation for meaning negotiation: meanings have non-linguistic effects

Avoiding verbal disputes isn't the only reason for engaging in meaning negotiation. How we define terms in context (e.g. how we let context fix meaning and/or which context we find ourselves in) has important effects on non-linguistic aspects of our lives. Here are some examples to illustrate what we have in mind:

Consider first the dispute above about how to use the term 'rich'. We said that Didi and Naomi disagree about what counts as a luxury, what counts as a necessity, and what counts as having significantly more than average wealth. This illustrates an important point: we take rich people to have luxuries, to have more than what they need, and to have significantly more wealth than average people. Of course, if we have those expectations, then *we might treat those people differently.* We have different expectations of them and we behave differently towards them. It affects our non-linguistic behavior.

The point just made applies to a very wide range of expressions, but here are some very dramatic cases to make the point. Consider first the meaning of the word 'person'. According to the 14th Amendment to the US Constitution, states may not 'deprive any person of life, liberty, property, without due process of law, nor deny any person within its jurisdiction equal protection of the laws'. What does 'person' mean in that context? More generally, what does it mean in a legal context? 'Person' is a vague term and the borderline cases can be settled in different ways. It is a matter of accommodation and negotiation. Needless to say, there has been very intense and highly public disagreement about what the meaning of 'person' should be. Chapter 2 of Ludlow's (2014) *Living Words* provides a good overview of the abortion debate in the US, conceived of as an exercise in meaning negotiation. As Ludlow points out, in the Supreme Court case *Roe v. Wade*, the debate is explicitly presented as a discussion of how 'person' should be applied. Here are a selection of exchanges (quoted by Ludlow 2014: 58) between the anti-abortion attorney Robert Flowers and Justice White:

> THE COURT: Well, if you're correct that the fetus is a person, then I don't suppose you'd have—the State would have great trouble permitting an abortion, would it?
> MR. FLOWERS: Yes sir.
>
> THE COURT: The basic constitutional question, initially, is whether or not an unborn fetus is a person, isn't it?
> MR. FLOWERS: Yes, sir, and entitled to the constitutional protection.
>
> THE COURT: Do you think the case is over for you? You've lost your case, then, if the fetus or the embryo is not a person? Is that it?
> MR. FLOWERS: Yes sir, I would say so.

As Ludlow (2014: 57) also points out, Justice Blackmun emphasizes this point in the Supreme Court's ruling on the case:

If this suggestion of personhood is established, the appellant's case, of course, collapses, for the fetus' right to life would then be guaranteed specifically by the [Fourteenth] Amendment. (Blackmun 1973: 156–7)

The question we're concerned with here is why we should care about meaning negotiation—why the outcome of such disputes matters to us.

We've just seen an example where the significance is crystal clear and the practical implications immense. We also have an illustration of how varied the processes of negotiation can be. In this case, it was a public process involving a legal system, the political system, and extensive public debate. There are many examples of these kinds of very public and long-winded negotiations. Here are a few salient cases:

- What is a war? Is 'the war on drugs' or 'the war on terror' a war?
- What is a planet? Is Pluto a planet? (see Ludlow 2014: 42)
- What is an immigrant?
- What is poverty?
- What is a healthy lifestyle?

We could go on listing cases like these. Many of them have the following in common: they involve vague terms that have borderline cases and there is disagreement—in these cases, public disagreement—about how to draw more precise lines. Moreover, it matters a lot how the lines are drawn.

In the examples above we have construed 'context' very broadly, as something that persists a long time, involves many people, and takes place over many locations. This is different in many respects from the kind of negotiation that typically takes place in normal everyday conversation between people. In those cases, the format is often tacit (speakers are not aware that this is what they are doing) and quick (since conversations are over pretty quickly), and the mechanisms are difficult to pin down. Typically, the consequences of negotiation in everyday conversations are less dramatic. That, however, is not to say that they are insignificant—the cumulative effects of such negotiations can have large effects on our lives.

11.5 Meaning Negotiation and Asymmetrical Power Relations

So far we have considered some illustrations of meaning negotiation. They have been of very different kinds: some are public events that take place in courtrooms and in public debate over longer periods of time. Of course, most cases are not like that—in everyday conversations we don't file briefs or spend much time negotiating the meaning of 'every' or 'person' or any other term we use. That is not to say we don't do it. It is only to say that *if* we do it, it is largely a process we are unaware of. It happens quickly and is largely the result of processes that happen without a great deal of reflection. As of the writing of this book, there isn't much understanding of those processes. However, one point is worth emphasizing (c.f. Ludlow (2014)): Conversations often have asymmetrical power relations. One conversation partner is assumed to be conversationally dominant. It is not a well-understood phenomenon, but the structure and effect of the asymmetry is clear:

- Contexts are shaped by accommodation and negotiation
- Contexts shape what we say
- Some conversation participants have more conversational power than others
- As a consequence: those with more power have more influence over the meaning of the word relative to a context.

What does it take to be conversationally dominant? There is probably no complete, systematic, or general answer to this question. Here are some examples of ways someone might be conversationally dominant:

- By being more knowledgeable about the subject matter
- By being perceived as more knowledgeable (even if one isn't)
- By having more power in a non-linguistic sense (e.g. being a boss over an employee, teacher over a student, an expert over a layperson, an aggressive person with a gun over an unarmed victim, or a Supreme Court judge over an appeals court judge).

The list could go on and on. What is important about these cases is that having the power to shape contexts has important consequences, not just in the kind of spectacular public events like a Supreme Court decision, but also in ordinary day-to-day conversations or in a seminar room discussion. The power to shape contexts and so meanings of words can have small effects in everyday conversations, but these small effects can have immense consequences as they add up over time.

11.6 Asymmetrical Power Relations, Gender, Silencing, and Pornography

Rae Langton, Jennifer Hornsby, Ishani Maitra, and many others have appealed to the phenomenon of asymmetrical conversational power to illuminate gender inequalities and women's in ability to say what they want to say. A central notion in much of this literature is that of silencing. What follows is a brief introduction to that idea.

One obvious way in which a person can be silenced is to physically prevent them from speaking. That is the literal form of silencing—preventing someone from speaking in the first place. However, the form of silencing we now want to focus on is different. It is a form of silencing that takes the form of controlling the context in which speech is made and so controlling what is said in that context—i.e. controlling what counts as a correct interpretation in that context. We have already seen one important example of that: the correct interpretation of the 14th Amendment in a legal context is determined by a very small group of people—the Supreme Court Justices. In an important sense, that small group of people decide what the word 'person' means in the context of the US legal system. Here are two other examples of how controlling context can determine what can be said:

- Consider the claim that 'everyone has equal standing before the law'. An expression like 'everyone' is context sensitive. Its extension depends on the domain and the domain is picked out in context. If a group of people could control the context in such a way that the domain is restricted to, say, male property owners, that could have immense practical implications. Someone who was trying to say that everyone, irrespective of gender and financial standing, has equal standing before the law would be prevented from doing so (at least by using the sentence 'everyone has equal standing before the law' in that context).
- Consider a game kids sometimes play. This game creates a context in which everything a participant says means the opposite of what it normally means. So, for example, if Jill says: 'that's delicious', she says that the thing she's pointing at is disgusting. But now imagine that Jill wants to stop playing the game. So she says: 'I don't want to play anymore'. Then those playing can say: 'Okay, great—we'll keep going'. If she tries to say that she wants out of the game within the rules of the game, she has to say 'I want to keep playing'. But the problem with this strategy is twofold: a) she is in so doing still playing the game, and b) those in control of the context can decide to interpret Jill's utterance as a straight assertion (outside the game), and so there's no way for her to get out of the game.

The thought that power affects context was used by Langton and West (1999) to describe the effects of pornography as a form of silencing. Langton and West treat pornography as speech that introduces certain presuppositions into the context—these are presuppositions about women and their subordination to men. The asymmetrical power relations between men and women make it difficult for women to reject those presuppositions:

> We have suggested that pornography introduces certain presuppositions about women, that these presuppositions figure as a component of score in language games, and obey rules of accommodation. And we have seen that in general the moves one can make in a language game can depend upon one's position of relative power in that language game. Suppose that women are often comparatively powerless in sexual language games, and pornographers and men are often comparatively powerful. Suppose that men and women are participants in language games in which moves are highly sensitive to the relative power and authority of speakers. Our suggestion is that ... pornography affects the score of the sexual language game—a score which women cannot or do not adequately challenge. (Langton and West 1999: 313)

Langton and West go on to argue that these effects are then transferred to ordinary conversations between men and women and that the presuppositions introduced in pornographic language games are transferred into these normal contexts:

> The men who take part in pornographic conversations then take part in ordinary conversations with real women. Our suggestion is that the presuppositions introduced by the pornographic conversations persist in the conversations with real women. The result is that ... she may, for example, say 'no' in a sexual context, and her intended move of refusal may fail to count as correct play. She may utter words when testifying in court about a rape, and her intended move of describing a rape may fail to count as correct play. She may utter words of protest, but her intended move may fail to count as correct play. (Langton and West 1999: 313)

Roughly, if someone has the power to create a context in which uttering 'no' is a way to give consent, and where 'yes' is also a way to give consent, a situation has been created that is analogous to the child's 'opposite' game.

This line of thought has triggered a great deal of discussion over the last twenty years. Various ways of articulating silencing have been proposed and the specific claims about the effects of pornography have been discussed (see the further reading at the end of the chapter for additional literature and discussions).

11.7 Negotiation and Accommodation: Creating Reality or Creating Meaning?

So far we have treated accommodation and negotiation as processes that shape and create context for the speech that takes place in those contexts. Since contexts shape meanings, accommodation and negotiation are responsible for shaping contextual meanings.

We end this book with a brief sketch of an alternative perspective on accommodation and negotiation. Recall that at the beginning of Chapter 1 we said that our evidence showed that both love and 'love' are context sensitive. In other words, the evidence showed, we claimed, that both the word and the phenomenon itself exhibited sensitivity to context. The argument for this was simple:

Suppose the word 'love' is context sensitive. Now consider the question: What is love? One true, though not very informative, answer to that question is that *love is whatever is picked out by the expression 'love'* (in English). But if 'love' is context sensitive, then what is picked out varies between contexts. If so, there isn't *one* thing that is love—the nature of love varies, in some important sense, between contexts.

This line of thought can be applied to many of the context-sensitive expressions we have discussed throughout this book (though see Question 1 at the end of the chapter for some reservations). In particular, it applies very straightforwardly to the kinds of expression that are subject to negotiation and accommodation. Consider three of the examples discussed above: some expressions like 'marriage', 'war', and 'immigrant' are subject to extended public negotiation. There is no agreement about what those words should cover and negotiation over the correct meaning involves a complex mix of political, legal, cultural, religious, and moral considerations. The kinds of expressions Lewis focused on are subject to negotiations within conversations more narrowly construed, e.g. between a few people over a short period of time. Even in these cases, the result of the negotiations can be of enormous significance. Think about negotiations over terms like 'selfish', 'well behaved' (as applied to a kid, for example), 'fair', 'too expensive', 'brilliant' (applied to a student or a job candidate) or 'lazy'. These terms don't come with fixed, contextually immovable meanings. One conversational participant can propose a use where you are accurately described by one of those terms, but other participants can resist the application. In many such cases, they are not disagreeing about the facts, but disagreeing about how the terms should be used in that context.

Let's focus on two cases: the extensive public negotiation over the expression 'marriage' and a more narrow negotiation over 'lazy' as applied to a particular individual in a particular conversation. The negotiations determine what 'marriage' and 'lazy' apply to (in the respective contexts). But marriage and laziness, in those contexts, just are what those terms apply to. So one natural description of the negotiations is the following:

> The conversational participants are negotiating what marriage and laziness are. The outcome of those conversations fixes not just something about language, but also something about the world: the kinds of things marriage and laziness are.

In other words, one way to describe the process of negotiation and accommodation is as a worldly matter: we are creating, for our particular purposes, aspects of the world. It is a way of world-creation.

With that point in mind, recall the points about asymmetrical power relations in linguistic negotiations that we made in the previous section. Some conversations partners have more influence on linguistic negotiations than others. What that means, in the light of the points just made, is that they have more power to create the various features of reality (for the purpose of their respective contexts). Linguistic negotiations are also, in part, negotiations over what the world should be like, and those who win those negotiations have power to shape the world, not just the meaning of words.

CENTRAL POINTS IN CHAPTER 11

- Accommodation is a process through which speech creates context.
- David Lewis formulated various rules of accommodation.
- When audiences don't accommodate, they can engage in linguistic negotiation.
- Linguistic negotiations can be affected by asymmetrical power relations.
- Linguistic negotiation is a way of constructing parts of the world—they are expressions of what the world should be like.

> QUESTIONS FOR CHAPTER 11

Comprehension Questions

11.1. If I say 'I hereby marry you', then straightway has a change been made in my status in the institution of marriages that differs from accommodation?

11.2. Think of a conversation you had recently that involved accommodation and negotiation.

11.3. Can you think of other things like pornography that similarly serve to silence? What about sexist comedy?

11.4. What should we do about pornography, if it plays the pernicious role which we've argued that it does?

Exploratory Questions

11.5. a) What, if any, are the presuppositions that are introduced by pornography (and in particular, does that question have a general answer)?

b) Do these presuppositions persist across conversations, as assumed by Langton and West?

11.6. Are accommodation and negotiation involved in the interpretation of basic indexicals, such as 'now', 'here', 'that', etc.? Consider three cases:

a) 'That is red' (pointing at a fruit that is red on the inside, not outside): Can accommodation be applied to both 'that' and 'red'?

b) 'We must leave now' (that very second? Within two minutes or that day or that year or within some reasonable time period? Can the correct interpretation of 'now' be subject to accommodation?

c) Finally, consider this case from Alex Silk (2014: 17). Women got the right to vote in the US after the amendment of the nineteenth amendment to the US Constitution. Now imagine Chip speaking before the ratification. He says: 'Isn't America great! Everyone can vote.' Suppose, in context, Chip takes 'everyone' to be contextually restricted to 'everyone who has a moral right to vote' so that the claim he tries to make is: *everyone who has a moral right to vote has a legal right to vote*. There are two ways we can object to Chip: we can object to the claim—i.e. disagree with his implication that women don't have a moral right to vote. Alternatively, we can object to the contextual restriction—we can just refuse to accommodate that restriction. How would we adjudicate between those options?

> FURTHER READING FOR CHAPTER 11

There's a lot of literature on accommodation. Lewis' (1979) is the classic reference; some useful references are in Beaver and Geurts (2011).

For meaning negotiation, see Hornsby and Langton (1998), Ludlow (2014), Plunkett and Sundell (2013), and Moravcsik (1990).

For issues such as silencing see Saul (2006) and Maitra (2009).

Bibliography

(Note: 'SEP' stands for Stanford Encyclopedia of Philosophy, available freely here: plato.stanford.edu)

Almog, Joseph, John Perry, and Howard Wettstein. (1989). *Themes From Kaplan*. Oxford University Press.

Anand, Pranav and Andrew Nevins. (2004). "Shifty operators in changing context". In *Proceedings of SALT 14*.

Austin, John L. (1962). *Sense and Sensibilia*. Oxford University Press.

Bach, Kent. (2004). "Pragmatics and the Philosophy of Language". In L. Horn and G. Ward (eds.), *The Handbook of Pragmatics*, Wiley-Blackwell. 463–87.

Bach, Kent. (2006). The excluded middle: Semantic minimalism without minimal propositions. *Philosophy and Phenomenological Research* 73 (2): 435–42.

Beaver, David and Bart Geurts. (2011). "Presupposition", in SEP.

Bennett, Jonathan. (2003). *A Philosophical Guide to Conditionals*. Oxford University Press.

Bezuidenhout, Anne. (2002). "Truth-Conditional Pragmatics". *Noûs* 36(s16): 105–34.

Bianchi, Claudia. (2003). "How to Refer: Objective Context vs Intentional Context". In P. Blackburn, C. Ghidini, R. Turner, and F. Giunchiglia (eds.), *Proceedings of the Fourth International and Interdisciplinary Conference On Modeling and Using Context (Context'03), Lecture Notes in Artificial Intelligence*, Volume 2680. Springer-Verlag.

Borg, Emma. (2006). *Minimal Semantics*. Oxford University Press.

Braun, David. (2015). "Indexicals", in SEP.

Braun, David and Ted Sider. (2007). "Vague, So Untrue". *Noûs* 41: 133–56.

Brogaard, Berit. (2012). *Transient Truths: An Essay in the Metaphysics of Propositions*. Oxford University Press.

Cappelen, Herman and Ernest Lepore. (2006). "Shared Content". In B. Smith and E. Lepore (eds.), *Oxford Handbook of Philosophy of Language*, Oxford University Press.

Cappelen, Herman. (2008a). *"Content Relativism" Relative Truth*. Oxford University Press (eds. Manuel García-Carpintero and Max Kolbel).

Cappelen, Herman. (2008b). "The Creative Interpreter: Content Relativism and Assertion". *Philosophical Perspectives* 22.1: 23–46.

Cappelen, Herman and Josh Dever. (forthcoming). *Relativism* (Introductions to Contemporary Philosophy of Language, Oxford University Press).

Cappelen, Herman and John Hawthorne. (2009). *Relativism and Monadic Truth*. Oxford University Press.
Cappelen, Herman and Torfinn Huvenes. (forthcoming). "Relative Truth". In Michael Glanzberg (ed.), *Oxford Handbook of Truth*, Oxford University Press.
Cappelen, Herman and Ernest Lepore. (2005). *Insensitive Semantics*. Oxford University Press.
Cappelen, Herman and Ernest Lepore. (2012). *Language Turned On Itself: The Semantics and Pragmatics of Metalinguistic Discourse*. Oxford University Press.
Caplan, Ben. (2003). "Putting Things in Contexts". *Philosophical Review* 112: 191–214.
Carston, Robyn. (2002). *Thoughts and Utterances: The Pragmatics of Explicit Communication*. Oxford: Blackwell.
Chalmers, David. (2011). "Verbal Disputes". *Philosophical Review* 120(4): 515–66.
Chierchia, Gennaro and Sally McConnell-Ginet. (2000). *Meaning and Grammar: An Introduction to Semantics*. MIT Press.
Cohen, Jonathan and Eliot Michaelson. (2013). "Indexicality and the Answering Machine Paradox". *Philosophy Compass* 8(6): 580–92.
Cohen, Stewart. (1999). "Contextualism, Skepticism, and the Structure of Reasons". *Philosophical Perspectives* 13(s13): 57–89.
Cohen, Stewart. (forthcoming). "Theorizing about the Epistemic". *Inquiry*.
Davidson, Donald. (1967). "Truth and Meaning". *Synthese* 17: 304–23.
Davies, Martin and Lloyd Humberstone. (1980). "Two Notions of Necessity". *Philosophical Studies* 38(1): 1–31.
Davis, Wayne. (2013). "Dyadic contextualism and content relativism". *Intercultural Pragmatics* 10.1: 1–39.
Edgington, Dorothy. (1995). "On conditionals." *Mind* 104 (414): 235–329.
Egan, Andy. (2009). "Billboards, Bombs, and Shotgun Weddings". *Synthese* 166 (2): 251–79.
Egan, Andy, John Hawthorne, and Brian Weatherson. (2005). "Epistemic Modals in Context". In G. Preyer and G. Peter (eds.), *Contextualism in Philosophy*, Oxford University Press. 131–70.
Egan, Andy and Brian Weatherson. (2011). *Epistemic Modality*. Oxford University Press.
Evans, Gareth. (1985). "Does Tense Logic Rest on a Mistake?". In G. Evans (ed.), *Collected Papers*, Oxford University Press. 343–63.
Finkbeiner, Rita, Jörg Meibauer, and Petra Schumacher. (2012). *What is a Context? Linguistic Approaches and Challenges*. John Benjamins Publishing Co.
von Fintel, Kai and Anthony S. Gillies. (2008). "CIA Leaks". *Philosophical Review* 117: 77–98.

García-Carpintero, Manuel and Josep Macia. (2006). *Two-Dimensional Semantics*. Oxford University Press.

Gauker, Christopher. (1998). "What Is a Context of Utterance?" *Philosophical Studies* 91: 149–72.

Gauker, Christopher. (2008). "Zero Tolerance for Pragmatics". *Synthese* 165(3): 359–71.

Glanzberg, Michael. (2011). "More on Operators and Tense". *Analysis* 71: 112–23.

Goodman, Nelson. (1947). "The Problem of Counterfactual Conditionals". *Journal of Philosophy* 44: 113–20.

Greenberg, Mark and Gilbert Harman. (2008). "Conceptual Role Semantics". In E. Lepore and B. Smith (eds.), *The Oxford Handbook of Philosophy of Language*, Oxford University Press. 295–322.

Grice, Paul. (1989). *Studies in the Way of Words*. Harvard University Press.

Hart, H. L. A., and Honoré, A. M. (1959). *Causation in the Law*, Oxford Clarendon Press.

Hawthorne, John. (2006). "Testing for Context-Dependence". *Philosophy and Phenomenological Research* 73(2): 443–50.

Hawthorne, John and Ofra Magidor. (2009). "Assertion, Context, and Epistemic Accessibility". *Mind* 118(470): 377–97.

Heim, Irene. (1982). The Semantics of Definite and Indefinite Noun Phrases. PhD Dissertation, U. Mass.

Heim, Irene and Angelika Kratzer. (1998). *Semantics in Generative Grammar*. Blackwell.

Heim, Irene. (n.d.) Lecture Notes on Indexicality http://web.mit.edu/24.954/www/files/ind_notes.html Accessed 24th December 2015.

Heck, Richard. (2002). "Do Demonstratives Have Senses?" *Philosophers Imprint* 2(2): 1–33.

Holton, Richard. (2003). "David Lewis's Philosophy of Language". *Mind and Language* 18: 286–95.

Horwich, Paul. (1998). *Meaning*. Oxford University Press.

Humberstone, Lloyd. (2006). "Sufficiency and Excess". *Proceedings of the Aristotelian Society* 106(1): 265–320.

Jenkins, C. S. I. (2014). "Merely Verbal Disputes". *Erkenntnis* 79(1): 11–30.

Kamp, Hans. (1971). "Formal Properties of 'Now'". *Theoria* 37(3): 227–74.

Kamp, Hans. (1981). "A Theory of Truth and Semantic Representation". Reprinted in P. Portner and B. Partee (eds.), *Formal Semantics: The Essential Readings*, Blackwell.

Kaplan, David. (1970). "Dthat". *Syntax and Semantics* 9: 221–43.

Kaplan, David. (1977/1989). "Demonstratives". In Joseph Almog, John Perry, and Howard Wettstein (eds.), *Themes from Kaplan*, Oxford University Press. 481–563.

Kennedy, Christopher. (1997). *Projecting the Adjective*. PhD thesis, UC Santa Cruz.
King, Jeffrey. (2003). "Tense, Modality, and Semantic Values". *Philosophical Perspectives* 17: 195–245.
King, Jeffrey. (2011). "Structured Propositions", in SEP.
King, Jeffrey. (2014). "Speaker Intentions in Context". *Noûs* 48(2): 219–37.
King, Jeffrey, Scott Soames, and Jeff Speaks. (2014). *New Thinking about Propositions*. Oxford University Press.
Koelbel, Max. (2002). *Truth Without Objectivity*. London: Routledge.
Korta, Kepa and John Perry. (2015). "Pragmatics", in SEP.
Kratzer, Angelika. (1981). "The Notional Category of Modality". In H. J. Eikmeyer and H. Rieser (eds.), *Words, Worlds, and Contexts: New Approaches in Word Semantics*, Berlin: de Gruyter. 38–74.
Kratzer, Angelika. (1991). "Conditionals". In A. von Sechow and D. Wunderlich (eds.), *Semantik/Semantics: International Handbook of Contemporary Research*, Berlin: de Gruyter. 651–6.
Kratzer, Angelika. (2012). Modals and Conditions, Oxford University Press.
Kripke, Saul. (1980). *Naming and Necessity*. Harvard University Press.
Langton, Rae and Hornsby, Jennifer. (1998). "Free speech and illocution" *Legal Theory* 4 (1): 21–37.
Langton, Rae and Caroline West. (1999). "Scorekeeping in a Pornographic Language Game". *Australasian Journal of Philosophy* 77(3): 303–19.
LaPorte, Joseph. (2006). "Rigid Designators", in SEP.
Larson, Richard and Gabriel Segal. (1995). *Knowledge of Meaning*. The MIT Press.
Lasersohn, Peter. (2005). "Context Dependence, Disagreement and Predicates of Personal Taste". *Linguistics and Philosophy* 28(6): 643–86.
Lepore, Ernest and Herman Cappelen. (2005). *Insensitive Semantics: A Defense of Semantic Minimalism and Speech Act Pluralism*. Blackwell.
Leslie, Sarah-Jane. (2007). "Moderately Sensitive Semantics". In G. Preyer (ed.), *Context Sensitivity and Semantic Minimalism: Essays on Semantics and Pragmatics*, Oxford University Press.
Lewis, David. (1973). *Counterfactuals*. Blackwell.
Lewis, David. (1979). "Scorekeeping in a Language Game". *Journal of Philosophical Logic* 8(1): 339–59.
Lewis, David. (1980). "Index, Context, and Content". In S. Kanger and S. Öhman (eds.), *Philosophy and Grammar*, Reidel. 79–100.
Lewis, David. (1987). "Causation" in *Philosophical Papers*: Volume II. OUP: 159–71.
Lewis, David. (1996). "Elusive Knowledge". *Australasian Journal of Philosophy* 74 (4): 549–67.
Ludlow, Peter. (2014). *Living Words*. Oxford University Press.

MacFarlane, John. (2005). "Making Sense of Relative Truth". *Proceedings of the Aristotelian Society* 105: 321–39.

MacFarlane, John. (2014). *Assessment Sensitivity: Relative Truth and its Applications*. Oxford University Press.

Maier, Emar. (2014). "Mixed Quotation: The Grammar of Apparently Transparent Opacity". *Semantics & Pragmatics* 7(7): 1–67.

Maitra, Ishani. (2009). "Silencing Speech". *Canadian Journal of Philosophy* 39(2): 309–38.

McGrath, Matthew. (2012). "Propositions", in SEP.

Menzies, Peter. (2004). "Difference-Making in Context." *Causation and Counterfactuals*, eds. Collins, Hall, and Paul: 139–80. MIT Press.

Moravcsik, Julius. (1990). *Thought and Language*. New York: Routledge.

Ninan, Dilip. (2010). "Semantics and the Objects of Assertion". *Linguistics and Philosophy* 33(5): 355–80.

Nunberg, Geoffrey. (2004). "Descriptive Indexicals and Indexical Descriptions". In Anne Bezuidenhout and Marga Reimer (eds.), *Descriptions and Beyond*, Oxford University Press. 261–79.

Pagin, Peter and Dag Westerståhl. (2010). "Compositionality I: Definitions and Variants". *Philosophy Compass* 5.3: 250–64.

Partee, Barbara. (1973). "Some Structural Analogies Between Tenses and Pronouns in English". *Journal of Philosophy* 70: 601–9.

Paul, L. A. & Hall, Ned. (2013). *Causation: A User's Guide*. Oxford University Press.

Perry, John. (2001). *Reference and Reflexivity*. Stanford: CSLI Publications.

Plunkett, David and Timothy Sundell. (2013). "Disagreement and the Semantics of Normative and Evaluative Terms". *Philosophers' Imprint* 13(23).

Potts, Christopher. (2005). *The Logic of Conventional Implicatures*. Oxford University Press.

Predelli, Stefano. (1998). "I am not here now". *Analysis* 58(2): 107–15.

Quine, W. V. O. (1960). *Word and Object*. The MIT Press.

Recanati, François. (2001). "Open Quotation". *Mind* 110: 637–87.

Recanati, François. (2004). *Literal Meaning*. Cambridge University Press.

Reimer, Marga. (1998). "What is Meant by 'What is Said'? A Reply to Cappelen and Lepore". *Mind and Language* 13(4): 598–604.

Richard, Mark. (2004). "Contextualism and Relativism". *Philosophical Studies* 119(1–2): 215–42.

Richard, Mark. (2008). *When Truth Gives Out*. Oxford University Press.

Rysiew, Patrick. (2011). "Epistemic Contextualism," in SEP.

Saul, Jennifer. (2006). "Pornography, Speech Acts, and Context". *Proceedings of the Aristotelian Society* 106(2): 227–46.

Schaffer, Jonathan. (2012). "Causal Contextualisms." In Martijn Blaauw (ed.), *Contrastivism in Philosophy: New Perspectives*. Routledge.

Schlenker, Philippe. (2003). "A Plea for Monsters". *Linguistics and Philosophy* 26 (1): 29–120.

Schroeter, Laura. (2012). "Two-Dimensional Semantics", in SEP.

Searle, John. (1980). "The Background of Meaning". In J. R. Searle, F. Kiefer, and M. Bierwisch (eds.), *Speech Act Theory and Pragmatics*, Dordrecht: D. Reidel Publishing Company. 221–32.

Sennet, Adam and Ernest Lepore. (2010). "Saying and Agreeing". *Mind and Language* 25(5): 583–601.

Silk, Alex. (2014). Discourse and Contextualism: A Framework for Contextual Semantics and Pragmatics. Manuscript.

Soames, S. (2005). *Reference and Description: The Case Against Two-Dimensionalism*. Princeton University Press.

Soames, Scott. (2006). "Understanding Assertion". In J. Thomson and A. Byrne (eds.), *Content and Modality: Themes From the Philosophy of Robert Stalnaker*, Oxford University Press. 222–50.

Soames, Scott. (2011). "Truth At". *Analysis* 71(1): 124–33.

Sperber, Dan and Deirdre Wilson. (1995). *Relevance*. Blackwell.

Stalnaker, Robert. (1978). "Assertion". Syntax and Semantics 9(315): 332.

Stalnaker, Robert. (2014). *Context*. Oxford University Press.

Stokke, Andreas. (2010). "Intention-Sensitive Semantics". *Synthese* 175(3): 383–404.

Travis, Charles. (1996). "Meaning's Role in Truth". *Mind* 105(419): 451–66.

Velleman, J. David. (2013). *Foundations for Moral Relativism*. OpenBook Publishers.

Williamson, Timothy. (2005). "Knowledge, Context and Agent's Point of View". In G. Preyer and G. Peter (eds.), *Contextualism in Philosophy*. Oxford University Press. 91–114.

Wettstein, Howard. (1981). "Demonstrative Reference and Definite Descriptions". *Philosophical Studies* 40(2): 241–57.

Index

Accommodation 174, 177–80
  and creating reality 188–9
Answering machine 160–2
Austin, J. L. 180

Basic set
  see Context Sensitivity: the Basic Set
Billboard example 170

Cappelen, H. and Lepore, E. 44–5, 49, 55–6
'Can' 178
Causation 19
Chalmers, D. 182
Character/Content distinction
  agreement data 90
  Cognitive significance 91–2
  Introduction 88
  and rigidity 94–6
  see also: Monsters, Kaplan, Kaplanian theory of meaning
Cohen, S. 21
Compositionality 71–4
Content Externalism 138
Context
  Introduction 1, 27
  and demonstratives 159–60
  determination question 153, 159
  global versus local 173–4
  High-Structure view 154
  and demonstratives 155–60
  and the determination question 159, 161
  improper 160–2
  ingredients of 164–74
  Kaplanian Context 101
  Low-structure view 154
  and the possession question 159, 161–2
  possession question 153, 159
  shiftable versus stable 122–4
  speaker versus audience 170–1
  of utterance versus of assessment 125
  see also: accommodation, negotiation

Context-Sensitivity
  and Ambiguity 14
  examples 11–20
  Introduction 6–9
  Philosophical significance of 23–4
  Puzzle of compatibility with Stability 41–2
  and rigidity 94–6
  and the semantics-pragmatics distinction 79–82
  The basic set 7–10, 37
  and vagueness 15–16
  Varieties of 25–6
Context shifting argument: 7–22, 97
Contextual parasites 45–8
  Problems 48–50
Counterfactuals
  and context-sensitivity 18–19
  and rigidity 78

Demonstratives 154–60
Diagonalization 142–6

Egan A,. 170
Egan, A., Hawthorne, J., and Weatherson, B., 168–9
Epistemic Modals
  and context 168–9
  and context-sensitivity 20
  and rigidity 78

Flight cases 21
Friendship 15–16

Games
  Analogy with conversation 177–80
  Opposites game 186
Gradable adjectives 16–17, 165–7

Hart, H. L. A. and Honoré, A. 19
Hawthorne, J. and Cappelen, H. 49
Holton, R. 178
Hornsby, J. 185
Humberstone, L. 315–16

INDEX

Indexed truth theory of
   meaning 110–14
   and diagonalization 142–6
   difference from Kaplanian theory 112
   double-indexing 122–5
   problem of rigidity 115–17, 124–6
   problem of same-saying 114–15, 133–47
Intensions and extensions
   and character 89
   Introduction 70–1
   see also: rigidity, compositionality, truth condition
Implication 75–7
   see also: truth conditions

Kaplanian theory of meaning 87–9, 106–7
   and compositionally 107–8
   explanation of context sensitivity 88–9
   and monsters 96–8
   operator argument 106–10
   see also: character content distinction
King, J. 157–8
Knowledge 20–2
Kratzer, A. 20, 179–80
Kripke, S.
   rigid and non-rigid terms 79

Langton, R. 185–7
Lewis, D.
   indexed truth theory of meaning 105
   on accommodation 177–80
   operator argument 111
   same-saying-scepticism 134–8
Love 13–14, 188
Ludlow, P. 183–4

Maitra, I. 185
Methodology 128–9
   and formal frameworks 147–8
   bottom-up 162
   see also: semantics and pragmatics, intension and extension, compositionally
'Might'
   see: epistemic modals
Minimalism 50–9
   and same-saying scepticism 137
   Mysterious 55–6
   Nihilistic 54–5
   Relativistic 56–9
   Weak 53–4

Monsters
   and double indexing 126–9
   and Kaplanian theory of meaning 96–8
   argument for existence of 98–101

Naked mole rat 41, 50, 155
Negotiation 180
   and non-linguistic effects 182–4
   and power 184–5

Operator 108–9
Operator argument 106–10

Parasites: *see* Contextual Parasites
Pornography 187
Possible worlds 68–71
Presupposition 171–4
Puzzle of compatibility of Context-Sensitivity and Stability 41–2

Radical contextualism 22–3, 44
   and same-saying scepticism 137–8
Richard, M. 180–1
Rigidity
   and Kaplanian theory of meaning 89, 94–6
Rigid versus non-rigid terms 77–9
   see also: Intensions and extensions, character-content distinction, indexed truth theory of meaning: problem of rigidity

Same-saying scepticism 133–47
Schlenker, J. 98
Semantics and pragmatics 79–82
   Dynamic pragmatics 146–7 *see also*: Presupposition
Shaquille O'Neal 77
Silencing 185–7
Similarity of Content 42–5
   Problems 44–5
Speech reports 36–8
   direct versus indirect 38
Stability
   Arguments against 42–5
   Arguments for 32–9
   Introduction 32
   Puzzle of compatibility with Context-sensitivity 41–2
Stalnaker, R. 105, 138–47
Subjective contextualism 138–42

Theory of Meaning
   and compositionality 71–4

and truth conditions 66–8
Introduction 65–6
see also: semantics and pragmatics
Truth Conditions 66–8
  and consequences 75–7
  and possible worlds 68–71

Venice beach example 157–8
Verbal disputes 181–2

What is said
  cognitive and communicative role 33–5
  context-Sensitivity of 9–10
  introduction 27–8
  and Kaplanian theory of
    meaning 88–9
  minimal 52–3
  and parasitism 47
  Pluralism about 51–2
  Pluralism versus
    monism 50–1
  scepticism about 134–8
  and truth conditions 66–8
Williamson, T. 15–16

'You' 169–71